EARLY CHILDHOOD EDUCATION FOR EVERY LEARNER

A UNIVERSAL DESIGN FOR LEARNING APPROACH

EARLY CHILDHOOD EDUCATION FOR EVERY LEARNER

Bweikia Foster Steen, EdD

© 2025 CAST, Inc.

All rights reserved. No part of this publication may be reproduced, stored in a retrieval system, or transmitted in any form or by any means, electronic, mechanical, photocopying, recording, or otherwise, without the prior permission of the Publisher.

ISBN (paperback): 978-1-943085-14-9
ISBN (ebook): 978-1-943085-15-6

Library of Congress Control Number: 2025937092

Cover and interior design by Happenstance Type-O-Rama

Published by CAST Professional Publishing, an imprint of CAST, Inc., Lynnfield, Massachusetts, USA

For information about special discounts for bulk purchases, please email publishing@cast.org or visit publishing.cast.org

CONTENTS

PART I: THE NEED

CHAPTER 1: Disrupting the Preschool-to-Prison Pipeline 3
CHAPTER 2: Braiding Antiracism and Universal Design for
Learning to Address the Peril 27

PART II: SETTING THE STAGE

CHAPTER 3: Creating a Welcoming Physical Environment 47
CHAPTER 4: Creating a Welcoming Culture and Climate 65
CHAPTER 5: Creating a Welcoming Temporal Environment. 77

PART III: APPLYING UDL FOR INCLUSIVE, ANTIRACIST RESULTS

CHAPTER 6: Applying UDL to Your Planning. 95
CHAPTER 7: The Uses of Assessment 121
CHAPTER 8: The Role of the Individualized Education Program . . 139
CHAPTER 9: Leveraging Technology Tools. 153
CHAPTER 10: Becoming a Reflective Educator 169

APPENDIX: Additional References for Educators 181

References 185
Index 199
About the Author 212

PART I

The Need

CHAPTER 1

Disrupting the Preschool-to-Prison Pipeline

DJ, a first grader, enthusiastically rushes through the doors and down the hall of his elementary school toward his classroom. Upon entry, his teacher greets him and asks, "Are you going to have a better day today and control your body?" DJ smiles, nods, and hurries to his assigned seat.

His teacher immediately begins to reflect on the previous school day's incidents. She has noticed that when he doesn't get an answer correct, or a friend doesn't play with him, feelings of embarrassment, shame, and loneliness trigger a negative response. He often runs out of the classroom, down the hall, and out the front doors of the school. DJ's teacher is aware that his parents are in the middle of a divorce and a custody battle. It seems that the frustration and anger he feels as he goes back and forth from one parent to the next throughout the week manifest during school hours. She is also aware that DJ is repeating first grade.

DJ's school norm consists of regular visits to the principal's office, exclusion from field trips and school events, calls home to his parents, and suspensions. At just 7 years old, he is already in the school-to-prison pipeline.

○ ○ ○

It's no secret that in the United States we are facing a crisis in our school systems. The policies and practices of many school systems across the country push racially, ethnically, and otherwise marginalized groups out of the schools and into criminal justice systems at alarming rates. These are groups that are systematically excluded or underrepresented in society, such as students with disabilities, ethnic and indigenous individuals (American Indian and Alaska Native, Asian, Black, Hispanic, and Native Hawaiian/Pacific Islander), LGBTQ+ students, and other communities. These students often face additional challenges, both in and out of the classroom, due to deeply ingrained social, cultural, and institutional biases. Addressing their needs requires intentional efforts to dismantle the systems of exclusion and to create inclusive, equitable learning environments that honor and support their identities and experiences. This crisis is commonly known as the *school-to-prison pipeline*, highlighting the correlation between academic processes that fail to engage, represent, or provide equitable opportunities for development and learning for racially and ethnically diverse students, the various exclusionary punishments (such as suspensions and expulsions) that are disproportionately applied to them, and the recipients of those punishments going on to be arrested and incarcerated (Adamu & Hogan, 2015; Bacher-Hicks et al., 2019).

The 2022 National Assessment of Educational Progress (NAEP), also known as the Nation's Report Card, indicates a general decline in math and reading scores compared to 2019, the previous assessment year (NAEP, 2022a; 2022b). But while the average fourth-grade math score for all racial groups decreased by 5 points, Black and Latino fourth graders in particular saw a sharper decline (an average of 7 points). Similarly, reading scores for Black and Brown (Latino, American Indian/Alaska Native, and Native Hawaiian/Other Pacific Islander) fourth-grade children declined by between 4 and 7 points in 2022 compared to an average of 3 points across racial groups. Less than 20% of Black and Brown fourth graders were assessed as proficient in reading or math. Although these losses were undoubtedly supercharged by the pandemic, the recently released data for the 2024 NAEP indicates that reading scores for Black and Brown children stagnated while math scores for Black and Latino fourth-graders recovered only slightly, showing an average increase of 3% compared to 2022 (NAEP, 2025a, 2025b).

These disadvantages during the early years of schooling have long-lasting, cumulative effects: one in six Latino, one in five Black, and one in four American Indian/Alaska Native public school students do not graduate on time (NCES, 2022). As educational progress has declined, there has also been an increase in the number of students aged 3 to 21 receiving services under the Individuals with Disabilities Education Act (IDEA), from 6.4 million in the 2012–13 school year to 7.5 million in 2022–23. Taken as a percentage of total public school enrollment, this equates to an increase from 13% to 15% of students. By race/ethnicity, the percentages of public school students served under IDEA in the 2022–23 school year was highest for American Indian/Alaska Native (19%) and Black (17%) students (NCES, 2024b).

While it is important to continuously analyze such data about outcomes, we also need to consider the barriers that prevent learning and development in the first place. These include attitudes toward learning, the contexts in which students learn, what resources are available, student time in school (attendance), and student confidence in subject matter knowledge. Such factors may contribute to students' feeling of unbelonging early in their educational careers (Watson, 2021). As the Children's Defense Fund's *State of America's Children* report (2023) observes, "the impact of exclusionary discipline policies, the continuous perpetuation of racist and inequitable systems and inadequate public investment, and the educational environments for our children and youth are creating barriers" that can potentially stand in the way of learning and development.

The conversation about the school-to-prison pipeline typically focuses on older students, in middle and high school. However, the funneling of children into this pipeline begins much earlier than that. The focus of this book will be on addressing the *preschool-to-prison pipeline*, also known as the *cradle-to-prison pipeline*, which calls attention to the disparities young Black children face in our school systems from as early as 3 and 4 years old. For instance, according to the Office for Civil Rights (USDOE, 2021), in the 2017–18 school year, Black preschoolers represented 18.2% of the total preschool population but accounted for 43.3% of students who received at least one out-of-school suspension. The disparity was particularly marked for Black preschool boys, who accounted for 9.6% of total enrollment but for 34.2% of students who received suspensions. Black preschoolers also received a disproportionate percentage of expulsions, at over two times more than their share of total enrollment. Put differently, Black preschoolers are expelled and suspended from preschool at more than two and three times the rate of their White counterparts, respectively.

Young racially and ethnically diverse students are also at risk of being disproportionately affected by events that disrupt schooling. The Northwest Evaluation Association (NWEA) found that during the COVID-19 pandemic, students experienced lower growth rates in math and reading than during a typical year. These declines had a disproportionate impact on Black, Latino, and American Indian/Alaska Native students and were particularly evident for students in grades 3–5 (Lewis et al., 2021). The Latino population, who can trace their heritage to a variety of Latin American countries, is the largest ethnic group of students in America's schools, accounting for 29% of the K–12 population as of 2022 (NCES, 2024a). These students—about 94% of whom are U.S.-born citizens—had seen decades of steady increases in assessment scores in reading and math, but this positive trend was threatened by the pandemic, whose harmful effects on the educational progress of children in grades 3–8 were felt most strongly in the high-poverty schools that Latino children are more likely to attend (UnidosUS, 2022).

The time young children spend in the school environment helps to form their opinions about themselves and about education and school in general. As Zaretta Hammond (2014) states: "Many children start school with small learning gaps, but as they progress through school, the gap between African American and Latinx and White students grows" (p. 15). The earlier young students experience social and academic failure in school, the earlier they experience feelings of being left out, undervalued, or ignored (reinforced, perhaps, by suspensions and exclusions), the earlier they begin to feel discouraged and alienated by their academic experiences. Eventually, they will start to demonstrate their frustration at this unfair, inequitable treatment through their actions and behaviors and by mentally dropping out. Experiences such as repeated failures, embarrassments, or boredom deflate the joy many young children bring into the early childhood classroom and manifest as barriers that prevent positive development, learning, and effective preparation for the later academic grades.

Stated simply, the school experiences that our youngest learners have influence their thinking and actions (Kostelnik et al., 2019). When children have negative experiences as early as in prekindergarten, they risk losing the excitement for learning that they once had and developing negative opinions about school. Their sense of whether school is a safe place for them to grow and develop and their perception of their academic abilities is shaped during these early years. By the fourth grade, when learners typically begin to move from acquiring concrete skills like reading and writing to developing higher order thinking and abstract skills, many racially and ethnically diverse students who have had adverse early school experiences have all but physically dropped out. Many have mentally decided school is not for them before they even reach the upper elementary grades.

WHY EARLY LEARNING IS ESSENTIAL

All of a child's experiences in school—social, emotional, and academic—during the early childhood years, and the early childhood educators who help to influence these experiences, matter. Early childhood education is defined as any group program serving children from birth to age 8 (NAEYC, 1993). Effective early childhood educators are essential to ensuring that young learners have equitable access to high-quality learning and care environments (NAEYC, 2019).

All schools, serving all ages and grades, should be safe places; however, ensuring schools are safe places for development and learning during the early childhood years should be an especially high priority because the first five years are the most critical period of a child's life.

During this time, 90% of brain development occurs (Schiller, 1999; Conkbayir, 2017). Therefore, it is no surprise that early childhood educators lay the foundation for developmental and academic success. These years are formative for all learning domains: linguistic, cognitive, social and emotional, and physical. As Beth Meloy et al. (2019) write, "well-implemented programs support substantial early learning gains and can have lasting impacts throughout a child's school career" (p. v). In other words, high-quality early school experiences matter (IOM & NRC, 2015).

Consequently, early childhood schools and classrooms should be spaces where children are celebrated for the diversity of experiences they bring, not judged, punished, or ridiculed for the experiences or skills they have yet to acquire. An early learning environment must be a place where young children have vast opportunities to explore, engage, interact, and experiment. Young learners should have boundless opportunities to explore their surroundings, have new experiences, and gain knowledge through rich, innovative, engaging instruction and exposure to appropriate curriculum and instruction.

According to the National Association for the Education of Young Children (NAEYC, 2022), early educators need to embrace a *both/and* approach instead of an *either/or* approach, "committed both to providing equitable opportunities to learn [for] each and every child and to viewing all children as capable of achieving at a high level" (p. 8). Antiracist early educators accomplish this by intentionally creating an environment where the joy of learning is maintained and instilled in students and social and emotional skills are cultivated in a developmentally appropriate way (Conkbayir, 2017). Developmentally appropriate practices are defined as "methods that promote each child's optimal development and learning through a strengths-based, play-based approach to joyful, engaged learning" (NAEYC, 2020, p. 5). This approach acknowledges the strengths each child brings to the classroom and capitalizes on them to address the areas of concern, challenging one's own assumptions and beliefs.

Subsequently, the early school and classroom experiences—and the knowledge acquired during the early years—impact how young children engage with and contribute to the world around them. As NAEYC (2009) notes, "early experiences have profound effects, both cumulative and delayed, on a child's development and learning" (p. 12). When developmentally, culturally, linguistically, and ability-appropriate approaches are intentionally embedded within the early childhood classroom curriculum and environmental decisions, the joy and excitement young students enter the prekindergarten classroom with is retained and the barriers that prevent development and learning are reduced, if not eliminated.

With this approach, the curricula, instructional and assessment practices, and classroom environment do not perpetuate the injustices and inequities that, too often, permeate our school systems, but rather seek to intentionally and actively address the structural inequalities racially and ethnically diverse students commonly encounter during the early years of schooling.

INSTITUTIONAL RACISM: REASONS FOR THE PRESCHOOL-TO-PRISON PIPELINE

Racism is defined as "beliefs, attitudes, institutional agreements, and acts that tend to denigrate individuals and groups because of phenotypic characteristics or ethnic group affiliations" (Clark et al., 1999, p. 805). Institutional racism reinforces prejudices and injustices through patterns, resources, and expectations that are covertly or overtly embedded within policies, procedures, operations, and the climate and culture of public or private institutions (CARF, 1998). Such policies and practices, whether intentionally or not, produce outcomes that chronically favor one group of individuals over another, placing the latter at a disadvantage (Roundtable on Community Change, 2017). Institutional racism and discrimination impact the health, well-being, and learning of children by limiting access to resources, services, and supports that promote learning, well-being, and long-term stability (Iruka, 2022).

Institutional racism manifests for young children of color during the early years in the following ways:

- cultural expectations, biases, and prejudices
- disciplinary patterns
- resource distribution
- overidentification in special education

- trauma
- one-size-fits-all curricula

Let's take a look at each of these in turn.

Cultural Expectations and Prejudices

As Andratesha Fritzgerald (2020) states in her book *Antiracism and Universal Design for Learning*, young children of color experience racism before they are able to articulate and understand what they are experiencing. But that does not mean they are not aware that their situation is unfair and unjust. Too often, our young racial and ethnic minority students are punished for being children: for not knowing or understanding or abiding by the school's rules; for demonstrating what is perceived as "active" behavior, such as standing, dancing, walking around the classroom, or moving in their seats when the expectation from the teacher is that they sit still; for playing around when it's deemed inappropriate, fidgeting, falling out of their chairs, joking, and even talking too much. They are punished because of lack of cultural proficiency and because of stereotypes that center on the intersections of race, gender, and class, the families they come from, the languages they speak, the communities they live in, the experiences and the knowledge they have not yet acquired.

Institutional racism plays a leading role in perpetuating systemic and structural racism in institutions (like schools), through policies and practices that disadvantage specific students. Ana Rodriguez-Knutsen (2023) describes systemic or institutionalized racism as "the implicit or explicit rules and regulations within an organization that discriminate against marginalized communities," often manifesting as "bias for or against certain groups of people because of stereotypes based on their perceived race or ethnicity." The effects are observed in institutions ranging from healthcare to housing, education, and criminal justice. Structural racism, she observes, refers to "biased laws, policies, or practices that restrict people's access to services, opportunities, and resources because of their race," with compounding effects on family life, employment, mental and physical life, and beyond. Institutional racism is thus "a guiding principle that helps theorists across disciplines examine the systemic practices and policies that result in wealth, employment, housing, criminal justice, and political power disparities" (Toldson, 2020, p. 1).

When I taught first grade at a school in the San Francisco area, a colleague approached me to seek advice about a 6-year-old Black student in their class. The teacher described the child as talkative and suggested she needed to be tested for attention-deficit/hyperactivity disorder (ADHD). When I asked them to describe her characteristics, they stated that when called upon to answer questions, the little girl produced long, rambling replies, often taking 5 minutes to give her answer. I chuckled upon hearing the teacher's depiction because I, too, frequently find myself giving overly lengthy responses to questions due to my need to elaborate.

The difference between myself and the 6-year-old is that I have had decades to recognize and learn how to self-regulate my need to provide extensive, sometimes unnecessary detail. I explained to my colleague that the student was simply providing background information related to the topic. I also suggested activities and strategies they could use that would allow the child to feel successful and included within the classroom discussions—strategies that would model for all students how to shorten their response times and expand upon their ideas later, at more convenient times of the day.

In the scenario I just described, the teacher's lack of cultural proficiency and the child's lack of understanding of school rules and expectations could have led to this student being recommended for special education services, had the teacher not sought advice prior to submitting the paperwork. This type of scenario occurs frequently during the early years of education, and it can set up young diverse students for failure early in their academic careers. For this Black child, the decision to consider special services was based on the teacher's lack of knowledge about cultural and linguistic backgrounds and experiences that differed from her own. The child's excitement, joy, and simple desire to share more than what was perhaps warranted could have had a pernicious effect on her later academic career.

While some students can recover from such early school experiences, these experiences shape not only how they feel about school, but how they feel about themselves and how they perform in an educational setting. As a result, their self-esteem, social-emotional development, and mental picture of themselves as scholars can suffer permanent damage (James & Iruka, 2018). Those who fall socially, emotionally, and academically behind during their early years often remain academically behind for the duration of their academic careers. Low academic self-esteem is associated with institutional and structural racism, the policies and practices that signal to young students that they do not belong.

Discipline, Suspension, Expulsion, and Retention

Institutional racism informs policies and practices such as school policies on suspensions and expulsions, perpetuating inherent biases. Students at ages as young as 3 and 4 years old are already experiencing inequitable learning and developmental opportunities due to disproportionate application of disciplinary actions such as removal from the classroom, retention, suspension, and expulsion (Zeng et al., 2019). As discussed earlier, according to the Office for Civil Rights (USDOE, 2021), Black students account for the largest share of expulsions among preschool students (38.2% in the 2017–18 school year) and of preschoolers receiving one or more out-of-school suspensions (43.3%), despite making up less than a fifth of total enrollment.

Such early exclusionary school practices deprive young children of valuable learning experiences and have a negative impact on their self-esteem, school identity, and social-emotional development. They also leave a lasting negative impression on a child's views of the educational system.

Disciplinary processes historically have disproportionately penalized Black and Brown children. Inequitable school policies and practices have permeated our educational system, to the point where access to, experiences in, and outcomes during and after early learning differ widely due to race and skin color (Meek et al., 2020; Morris, 2022). Additionally, within the early childhood field, because of the various types of early care and education settings available to families, there is typically not one universal body that sets and enforces policies, practices, and procedures.

The lack of clearly defined and equitable processes and policies related to suspensions, retention, and expulsion within early care centers contributes to the preschool-to-prison pipeline. Young Black and Brown students may be sent out of the classroom, held back, suspended, and expelled for various reasons due to subjective practices that are built on racial disparities in school discipline practices. The U.S. Departments of Health and Human Services and Education issued a joint policy statement in 2014 urging early child care providers to establish policies and procedures that would work to eliminate the suspension of preschoolers; but whether overtly or unintentionally, such recommendations are often overlooked or simply ignored (Canty-Barnes, 2016).

Resource Distribution

As an early educator in a large elementary school in the San Francisco Bay area, I witnessed many injustices toward, in particular, Black children. I was one of two African American teachers out of over 50, and Black students made up 10% of the total school population. However, those students stood out due to the treatment they received. I can recall pushing back against and protesting the unfair treatment of two Black boys in particular: Dante and Charles, who were in first grade and would often roughhouse and play around during recess. Because of what was deemed unsafe recess behavior, they were instructed not to play with each other. Likewise, these two were often sent to the principal's office, spending time away from their classrooms, and were frequently not allowed to attend field trips because of their perceived negative behavior.

The next year, both boys were placed in my second-grade classroom. As I read each of their cumulative records, including files and documents provided by their previous grade's teacher, I noticed a glaring difference between what that teacher had written about these boys and the comments they had made about a White student in my class whose behavior was concerning me. Dante's and Charles's cumulative files each contained many pages of documented behavior reports, suspension reports, and student support team documents, whereas the White student's file included a one-sentence note that read: "Likes to misbehave because it's more fun."

This "discipline gap" also contributes to the preschool-to-prison pipeline. When young children are removed from the classroom for minutes, hours, or days, they lose valuable in-school opportunities to acquire social, emotional, and academic knowledge that they will need for later academic success. Likewise, when they are restricted from attending field trips, they miss out on valuable out-of-school experiences. When they are told who they can and cannot play with, they feel isolated. When they are told they cannot have recess, they are losing play time, which research has shown plays an important role in supporting children's social and emotional health (Kostelnik et al., 2019). These experiences, in isolation and cumulatively, contribute to low academic self-esteem and to the raising and perpetuation of barriers that prevent learning and development.

Black students are more than three times as likely as White students to be suspended or expelled from school, with differential treatment and support accounting for the largest share of this gap (Owens & McLanahan, 2020). Such disparities in the implementation of disciplinary policies and practices highlight the urgency of transforming early school experiences to ensure school readiness and school success. When our young students don't receive developmentally appropriate early starts, it makes it harder for them to attain societal goals such as strong math, reading, science, and other cognitive skills, and to acquire the abilities to collaborate and communicate effectively with others, complete assigned tasks, and solve problems creatively (García & Weiss, 2015).

It is also important to recognize that our young students are always watching and observing whether the policies, practices, and assessments applied to them are fair and equitable. They are watching to determine whether these policies and practices embrace their personalities, interests, and abilities, or whether instead they deny them access to the same experiences as their White peers. The messages they receive from their school and classroom environments (including teachers and staff) signal to them whether they belong and are valued, appreciated, and welcome to learn, or not. As stated earlier, they might not be able to articulate the reasons for the inequitable experiences, but they know that their experiences are not "fair."

As the Education Trust reports, another disciplinary measure that disproportionately impacts Black, Latino, and Native students (as well as English learners) is grade retention, a practice that without adequate support frequently leads to negative academic, social, and emotional outcomes over time (Davis, 2021). Despite these risks, students as young as 4 years old are commonly retained for reasons such as behavior, inability to self-regulate, lack of social-emotional development, lack of kindergarten readiness, and mismatches between school and home expectations. Aren't these the very skills early educators are supposed to model, prepare, and teach to all young students, because they are developmentally appropriate?

Grade retention and disciplinary actions such as removal from the classroom, suspension, and expulsion can lead students to feel isolated, unsupported, unheard, and unwelcome—and those feelings impact the desire to achieve. Sousa (2009) stated that "emotion drives attention and attention drives learning. But even more important to understand is that emotional attention comes before cognitive recognition" (p. 9). When students instinctively feel as though they don't belong, are not welcome, are treated unfairly or as an outsider, are powerless and/or vulnerable, their psychological defense mechanisms kick in. This desire to protect oneself and one's emotions frequently manifests in what is perceived as a negative attitude, an unwillingness to learn, and negative behavior. These children are identified early on as difficult and in need of being "fixed" (Adamu & Hogan, 2015; Novak, 2016). Such labels and identifications for Black and Brown students continue at disproportionate rates throughout the elementary and secondary levels.

Overidentification in Special Education

Policies, practices, and procedures that repeatedly misidentify and mislabel individuals in one group over another contribute to the overrepresentation of Black and Brown students within special education. Black students are the most overrepresented demographic (Garwood & Carrero, 2023; Morgan, 2020). This is especially disturbing because it signals an ongoing issue within our school systems that perpetuates low expectations, and a lack of knowledge related to resources available to assist with assessment, early intervention, and access.

The Individuals with Disabilities Education Act is a law that "makes available a free appropriate public education to eligible children with disabilities throughout the nation and ensures special education and related services to those children" (USDOE, n.d.-b). Additionally, the law is supposed to "ensure that educators and parents have the necessary tools to improve educational results for children with disabilities by supporting system improvement activities; coordinated research and personnel preparation; coordinated technical assistance, dissemination, and support; and technology development and media services" (USDOE, n.d.-b). However, the overrepresentation and overidentification of Black and Brown students in special education during the early years—in particular, among students served by IDEA (USDOE, 2024)—due to bias and cultural incongruence embedded within school policies, practices, and procedures has significant implications for how these students view themselves and how their academic identities are shaped. This effect is compounded by the fact that students served under IDEA are heavily overrepresented in disciplinary actions (USDOE, 2024).

Within the prekindergarten (3 years old) to third grade (8 years old) setting, young children are usually recommended to receive special education services by their teacher and/or a specialist. The identification process usually includes a team that consists of an administrator, a teacher, and a specialist who make decisions based on the assessments conducted. Racially, ethnically, and otherwise marginalized students are more likely than their White peers to be diagnosed with specific learning disability, mild intellectual disability, and emotional disturbance (Gatlin & Wilson, 2016). Each of these diagnoses is often associated with policies and practices that limit understanding of how to appropriately meet the developmental, cultural, linguistic, and individual needs of the students served; thus, they are labeled with social, emotional, and behavioral disorders.

Teachers' perception and interpretation of students' actions and behaviors is based largely on subjective beliefs and assumptions and can be affected by institutional racism that (perhaps unconsciously) influences their attitudes and judgments. The disparity in labeling of children as in need of special education may be improved by using a more individualized, culturally responsive and sensitive evaluation process, incorporating universal screening, response to intervention practices, and proactive and collaborative assessment practices that build on the strengths of the child rather than their deficits (NCLD, 2020).

Trauma

Adverse childhood experiences (ACEs) disproportionately impact diverse students. Early negative experiences within the school system, such as grade retention, suspension, and expulsion, can contribute to these experiences. ACEs are defined as stressful or traumatic events that occur prior to a child turning 18 years old; they include experiencing abuse (sexual, physical, or emotional), neglect (emotional or physical), discrimination, bullying, homelessness, and household dysfunction, including parental mental illness, incarceration, substance abuse, domestic and other forms of violence, and divorce. ACEs can have lasting, negative effects on well-being in childhood, and those impacts can last well into adulthood, affecting life opportunities (CDC, 2024). Said differently, ACEs can impact the developmental trajectory of young Black and Brown students.

Childhood trauma is defined as "a response to a negative external event or series of events which surpasses the child's ordinary coping skills" (McInerney & McKlindon, 2014, p. 1). In other words, trauma results from toxic stress and exposure to ACEs, which are perceived by the child as physically or emotionally harmful and/or threatening, and it can have lasting adverse effects on social, physical, emotional, academic, and spiritual well-being. Trauma symptoms can manifest across developmental domains, in the form of physical, cognitive, social-emotional, and language and literacy impairments (Statman-Weil, 2015). As H. Richard Milner et al. (2019) state, there is a direct link between trauma and academic performance and behavioral challenges, and "educators, unaware of trauma and its impact, may see these learning and behavioral challenges as disrespect, disabilities, or defiance, thus resulting in either inappropriate labeling of student ability or harsh disciplinary sanctions" (p. 40).

Throughout my years of teaching, I have found that although ACEs are often associated with factors related to the home and community environment, many racially and ethnically minoritized students suffer traumatic experiences while in the school setting due to disciplinary disproportionality, in the form of office discipline referrals, suspensions, expulsion, and even school arrests. A lack of recognition and understanding of the unintended consequences of ignorance, action, and inaction and how they perpetuate existing systems of privilege contributes to the prevalence of in-school and school-based trauma (NAEYC, 2019).

School-based trauma occurs due to racist practices that exclude, push out, and threaten the success of children of color and promote low academic self-esteem. It can be experienced as early as prekindergarten and ultimately influences learning outcomes and attitudes toward school, contributing to what is perceived as challenging behavior. School-based trauma affects the ability to learn and executive function skills because the child feels threatened, which then impacts their ability to cope (Erdman et al., 2020).

When a child has experienced school-based trauma, they may no longer trust the school setting. Misbehaving is often an unintentional reaction based on current and past experiences that have been perceived as threatening and required them to go into protection mode. These feelings of stress and mistrust fuel the impulse to mentally and sometimes physically drop out of school. Students suffering the symptoms of trauma from ACEs are especially at risk, often experiencing trouble concentrating, difficulty with learning tasks, or problems with memory (Bailey, 2014). This is because children who have experienced trauma are in a near-constant state of survival and protection mode.

Dr. Becky Bailey, creator of the Conscious Discipline approach, describes all behavior as a form of communication, and misbehavior as a call for help. She further explains that educators must realize that children who are expressing themselves through these behaviors have unmet needs and are missing the social and emotional skills required to express themselves (Bailey, 2014). Their pleas for help can be manifested in inappropriate behavior, which may then be misunderstood and characterized as insubordinate. To offer them the assistance they need, early educators must remain deliberately conscious of their biases as well as the multiple influences that may impact a child's development and learning.

Now, more than ever, classrooms are inundated with children who have experienced some form of trauma, whether school-based or out of school. As Anthony Rebora (2022) observes: "The pandemic, with its attendant disruptions and hardships, created new pressures and traumas for students." Its impacts on health, behavior, and social engagement opportunities highlighted the importance of prioritizing social and emotional development.

Because stressful or traumatic experiences can and do occur early in a child's life, it is imperative that early childhood and elementary school teachers are equipped with the basic knowledge, tools and strategies, and resources necessary to meet the social and emotional needs of these young students—which must happen before any learning can occur. More than ever, it is important to gain an understanding of trauma and its role in shaping behavior as we critically reflect on and evaluate our biases and how they inform the practices and policies that impact our diverse student populations during their early years.

How does trauma impact learning? As observed previously, emotion drives attention, and attention drives learning (Sousa, 2009, p. 9). The psychologist Robert Plutchik identified eight primary emotions, which he grouped into four opposing pairs: joy-sadness, anger-fear, trust-disgust, and surprise-anticipation. Secondary emotions are the feelings and reactions you project or have in response to the primary emotions and are often influenced by personal experiences, beliefs, and thoughts. These include anger, rage, shame, guilt, frustration, and sadness; they commonly mask other feelings and protect the self from being vulnerable (Table 1-1; Guy-Evans, 2023; Tull, 2020).

TABLE 1-1. Primary Versus Secondary Emotions

PRIMARY EMOTIONS	SECONDARY EMOTIONS
Joy-sadness	Anger, rage
Anger-fear	
Trust-disgust	Shame, guilt
Surprise-anticipation	Frustration, sadness

When a child's primary emotions—the original, direct emotional responses—are not addressed (that is, if an adult does not appropriately respond), the secondary emotions take over. Secondary emotions influence behavior, increase intensity of reactions, and last longer than primary emotions (Guy-Evans, 2023). In a school setting, this display will often result in disruptive behavior, lack of attention in class, or a refusal to participate, which leads to social, emotional, and academic failure.

Students who have experienced trauma may express themselves in several behavioral ways that need to be addressed. It is important to understand what those behaviors typically mean and employ strategies to help scaffold and model self-regulation. When faced with this situation, educators need to remember that children usually misbehave to signal that their basic needs have not been met. Furthermore, they may not trust that communicating their needs in typically acceptable ways will help (Fields et al., 2017, p. 37). In these instances, educators need to:

- Consider the child's age and use their understanding of child development to determine what behaviors are typical or atypical.
- Take into account the child's individual context (e.g., home life, nutrition, sleep patterns) and strive to understand the underlying reasons for their behavior.
- Analyze and interpret the available data objectively, avoiding subjective judgments based on assumptions or biases.
- Observe the child closely and build a relationship with them to identify their strengths, interest, talents, and abilities, which will help determine effective strategies.
- Consistently scaffold and respond to the child's needs.
- Demonstrate interest and positive feelings—being ignored makes children feel unimportant.
- Integrate predictable routines.

Table 1-2, while not comprehensive of all scenarios, suggests some ways to proceed.

Knowledgeable, antiracist teachers do not blame children, punish them for not doing work, or make them feel guilty for their behavior (Fields et al., 2017). They understand the importance of the early years in child development, and of developmentally appropriate guidance and practices. They recognize the vital role of assessing each child individually, in a developmentally, culturally, linguistically, and ability-appropriate way, and of meeting their present needs by appropriately modeling and scaffolding development and learning (that is, providing temporary supports that enable learners to "build knowledge or skills efficiently and enthusiastically" [Meyer et al., 2014, p. 109]). An antiracist early educator understands that "the brain of a child who has experienced trauma can be quick to perceive any reminder of it as a threat, whether or not it's actually threatening and whether or not she's consciously aware of it" (Kaiser & Rasminsky, 2021, p. 125). As early educators, we must continually strive to discern and reflect on every challenge in order to craft the best possible plan of action to meet the needs of each child.

TABLE 1-2. Behavior Has Meaning

IF A CHILD DISPLAYS THIS BEHAVIOR:	IT MAY MEAN THIS:	TRY THIS:
Shuts down	They are feeling **anxiety/anxious**. Think about: What causes the child to shut down? Are they shutting down because a primary emotion has not been addressed?	• Acknowledge the child and provide affirmations: I see you. I'm coming to help you. • Be consistent and calm. • Provide choices. • Eliminate embarrassment. • Provide opportunities for the child to teach other children. • Provide a safe space.
Resists learning	They are feeling **abandoned/alone**. Think about: What might be causing the child to resist learning? Are they really resisting learning, or is the task too easy or too hard?	• Acknowledge the child and provide affirmations: You worked for 5 minutes on this task. How can I help you with the next part of the task? • Provide a safe space. Include bean bag chairs or mermaid pillows, and a form they can complete that provides options they can circle to show what they need from their teacher (e.g., I need my teacher to provide: a hug, a walk, water, a visit to the counselor, a high five, help with my assignment). • Build a community/team. This can be a classroom community or a team that includes staff members.

(continued)

TABLE 1-2. Behavior Has Meaning (*continued*)

IF A CHILD DISPLAYS THIS BEHAVIOR:	IT MAY MEAN THIS:	TRY THIS:
Has an attitude	They are feeling **angry**. Think about: How can you develop a relationship with the child?	• Model. Think aloud: What were you thinking? What were you feeling? What did you do as a result? What other strategies could you use? • Ask the child about their strengths, talents, and hobbies outside of the school/classroom. Ask to attend an event. • Allow the child to draw what their mind is full of, or what were they thinking when they became angry. • Connect with the child. Be open and honest about your personal struggles or about times when you feel angry. • Provide alternative strategies: words to describe emotions, an emotions chart, a yoga center or mindfulness center.
Acts in a harmful or aggressive way, such as fighting	They are feeling **afraid**. Think about: What is the behavior trying to communicate?	• Find out the child's strengths and focus on those. • Co-regulate: model taking deep breaths or using yoga or mindfulness strategies. • Provide immediate positive feedback when the child is using the strategies discussed. • Relate: Share your strengths and weaknesses. • Ask the child to draw how they feel. • Be open and honest with the child about your struggles and the strategies you used to overcome them.

One-Size-Fits-All Curricula

As I have alluded to previously, one form of trauma nearly all students are dealing with today is the trauma from COVID-19. Thus, there is an urgent need to acknowledge ACEs and their link to behavioral challenges among students. This process must involve administrators and teachers striving to address institutional racism through systemic and proactive developmentally appropriate decisions, policies, and approaches to teaching. This in turn requires considering the individual needs of children and families and the appropriateness of the expectations and practices of administrators and teachers, as well as the relationships and interactions between them. By examining the curricula and instructional methods used in schools, we can create a more supportive environment that meets the diverse needs of all students.

Whether you teach in an early care center or in a K–3 setting, you will be required to teach a specific curriculum, which may dictate the expected instructional practices designed to accomplish desired goals. NAEYC (2022) states that "general knowledge of children's development and learning [helps] educators predict what goals are achievable . . . and what kinds of experiences and environments are most likely to support the achievement of those goals" (p. 12).

In my research, I have found that antiracist early educators recognize that the so-called "one-size-fits-all" approach does not appropriately meet the needs of individual students. In this approach, students are expected to know and meet "appropriate school norms and expectations." For example, they are expected to sit quietly in the classroom and to learn content at the same pace, using the exact same method, without any choice about how they are going to learn it or how they will express what they know (Novak, 2016). In my daughter's case, at 3 years old, she was reprimanded because she did not sit in criss-cross applesauce, neatly on the rug as the other girls in her classroom did. However, her prekindergarten teacher didn't expect the same behavior from the boys in the class. In fact, upon visiting one day to inquire about the concern I had related to my daughter's unfair treatment, I noticed that the teacher had made accommodations for a rambunctious White male student by allowing him to move around the classroom and sit in her lap when he wanted to, whereas my daughter was placed in the reading area by herself and expected to self-regulate.

Think about this: Have you ever tried on a shirt or pants that were supposed to fit all body sizes? In some cases, it might work; however, you most likely found that it was either too big or too small. In reality, the one size that supposedly fits all does *not* fit all. The same is true when it comes to young students, who enter the prekindergarten classroom with vastly varied experiences, exposures, abilities, and needs. Therefore, curriculum and instructional practices should not be scripted and prescribed to suit some predefined range. A scripted curriculum caters to the privileged. Those who don't have the expected experiences and background with the content are left out. Tell me, which policymaker or curriculum developer decided that all young children would need the exact same lesson at the exact same time, in the exact same way? Is that approach equitable? Does it focus on eliminating inequities to increase success for all groups?

When schools that serve racially, ethnically, and otherwise marginalized students adopt curriculum that is not developmentally appropriate and takes a one-size-fits-all, scripted approach, our young racially and ethnically diverse students are judged and assessed unfairly; thus, they suffer academically, and inequities persist. Ultimately, Pamela Cantor et al. (2021) state it best: "To achieve the transformation we need today, we must be willing to embrace what we know about how children learn and develop."

Utilizing a strengths-based approach helps to eliminate the barriers that stand in the way of learning and development. Such an approach recognizes that it is important to first engage students by creating opportunities for them to connect with their teachers and peers, thus encouraging them to experience positive emotions about the school environment and the content they are learning. This is done by gaining an understanding of child development, setting developmentally appropriate expectations, and taking the time to learn about the strengths and interests of each individual child. A strengths-based approach requires educators to focus attention on students' abilities rather than their shortcomings (Xie, 2013). Embracing young learners' funds of knowledge—their cultural practices, identities, ways of interacting, skills, and understandings—is also a vital step to applying a strengths-based approach (Moll et al., 1992).

What does trauma have to do with curriculum and instruction? As Justina Schlund (2021) notes, "Research has shown that we think and learn best when we have supportive relationships, feel a sense of security and belonging, and have opportunities to develop and practice our social, emotional, and cognitive skills across many different contexts." Learning does not occur without relationships that are built on mutual trust and respect. Thus, it is important to prioritize relationships that are built on developing the whole child by capitalizing on their strengths.

A one-size-fits-all approach to learning ignores the social contexts, customs, histories, experiences, and expectations of diverse communities and is typically premised on certain implicit biases and assumptions. This is dangerous because it leads to misconceptions and mismatches in expectations at home and at school that ultimately result in inequitable school policies and promote educational disparities. Instead of reflecting on the institutional racism that shapes the assumptions and biases of educators, which contribute to these disparities, the blame is often placed on students, their families, and their communities (Milner, 2019). A one-size-fits-all model that fails to utilize knowledge about child development to inform curriculum and instructional practices thus leads to the raising of barriers that prevent success for young students.

CONCLUSION

We cannot disentangle the intersectionality of the identities, cultures, languages, experiences, and abilities our young children bring to the early childhood context. Rather than trying to fit all students into a mold that is ill suited to so many of them, we should celebrate and support their diverse identities and experiences as providing motivation and a path to success. "It is our job to create ways of thinking, cultures, and personal relationships that make school a place of genuine belonging for every child" (Watson, 2021).

As reported by the Education Trust (Gillespie, 2019), early childhood education is essential to a strong early start in life—to the experiences, engagement, exposure, and access children need to become lifelong learners and to set them up for long-term success. Inequities exist at the earliest stages, leading to opportunity gaps that can be difficult to surmount. Institutional racism—the policies or behaviors within an organization that discriminate against people of color—must continually be watched for and addressed within our school systems to ensure equitable opportunities and experiences for racially and ethnically diverse students. Without this effort, the injustices and inequities it fuels will continue to compromise learning and development and contribute to the flow of the preschool-to-prison pipeline. We must seek to disrupt this flow by ensuring the diverse needs of students are met.

○ ○ ○

While driving during rush hour traffic in Washington, DC, I stopped at a red light behind a DC metro bus. On the back of the bus was a sign that read: "Knowledge is gained through experiences." It was as if I had an epiphany. Our young Black and Brown children are being punished for what they don't know; for their lack of understanding of experiences they have yet to encounter and limited exposure to specific or expected content knowledge; for school rules that differ from home rules, school expectations that differ from their cultural expectations, and high demands for self-regulation regardless of their young age.

I can remember showing my preschool-aged daughter a guava and asking her to identify the fruit. She replied, "Mommy, I don't know what that is."

Of course she couldn't identify the fruit; our family had never eaten guava before. It was her first exposure to it. My reaction was not to punish her for not knowing what it was, but to seek to teach her about it, using varied strategies. Contrary to my daughter's experience (or lack thereof) with the guava, the lack of exposure to relevant content and experiences for Black and Brown students often leads them straight into the preschool-to-prison pipeline.

I have since added additional words to my own version of the sign I saw on the back of that bus: "Knowledge is gained through intentional engagement, exposure, representation, action, and expression that allows all students the opportunity to appropriately develop, grow and learn." The development and learning of our Black and Brown students should remain the focus of all we do as early educators. Where there is a gap in learning, it is our obligation to assess and plan intentional curriculum and strategies to help build upon their current experiences and establish a stronger foundation for future growth.

CHAPTER 2

Braiding Antiracism and Universal Design for Learning to Address the Peril

While observing an intern in a public school second-grade classroom, I noticed that one little boy's name was called out more than those of any of the other children in the class. He was constantly being asked to sit next to the teacher or return to his desk to "take a break," or instructed to leave the classroom and stand outside the door. This young boy, who was Black, was eager to participate in the planned lessons. He would raise and wave his hands and shout out the answers, always getting them right but often being criticized for talking out of turn rather than rewarded. Naturally, I became interested in his social, emotional, and academic background and experiences.

Upon revisiting this classroom for a different observation of the intern, I asked her to provide some background information on this child and inquired about the support plans to meet his needs. She immediately stated that the boy was a behavior problem, but added that her mentor, the lead teacher, had a great relationship with him. The intern proceeded to describe the practices the lead teacher was using to promote positive development and learning opportunities for this student. For instance, it was noted that he needed frequent movement breaks; therefore, they rewarded him for sitting quietly on the carpet for 15 minutes during whole-group time with free time, when he could go outside and run around on the school's track for 15 minutes.

∘ ∘ ∘

As the previous chapter highlighted, institutional racism permeates our school systems and influences the policies and practices that govern decision making. Often, these decisions are informed by attitudes and behaviors that, instead of promoting equitable outcomes, perpetuate inequities that affect the outcomes of racially, ethnically, and otherwise marginalized children. For example, research by Phillip Goff et al. (2014) suggests that Black children are commonly viewed as older than they are, which leads to them experiencing age-inappropriate expectations and consequences. In addition, both Black and Brown children are viewed as more culpable for their actions than White children, and perceived culpability increases with perceived age. Thus, as Goff et al. observe, "children of all races may not be afforded the privilege of innocence equally" (p. 532), and "although most children are allowed to be innocent until adulthood, Black children may be perceived as innocent only until deemed suspicious" (p. 541).

Such beliefs and perceptions of children, both boys and girls, have an effect even during the early years and contribute to educational disparities. Thus, it is imperative that educators embrace frameworks and adopt effective practices that help them reflect on and recognize perceptions, viewpoints, and practices that maintain injustices.

This chapter will provide an overview of antiracism and its relationship to institutional racism, followed by a brief introduction to the principles of Universal Design for Learning (UDL). It will also explore the importance of prioritizing social-emotional development, creating a welcoming environment for all learners, and ensuring that their basic physiological and psychological needs are met in order to create the optimal conditions for learning. The concepts presented in this chapter can be used to support, with intentionality, rewriting the narrative of Black, Brown, and other racially and ethnically diverse children through reflection and implementation.

ANTIRACIST EDUCATION: DEFINITIONS AND PRINCIPLES

As Ibram Kendi writes:

> *The first step to building an antiracist America is acknowledging America's racist past. By acknowledging America's racist past, we can acknowledge America's racist present. In acknowledging America's racist present, we can work toward building an antiracist America. An antiracist America where no racial group has more or less, or is thought of as more or less. An antiracist America where the people no longer hate on racial groups or try to change racial groups. (Reynolds & Kendi, 2020, pp. xv–xvi)*

In his 2019 book *How to Be an Antiracist,* Kendi defines an antiracist as "one who is supporting an antiracist policy through their actions or expressing an antiracist idea" (p. 13). He further states that being an antiracist is an ongoing and difficult process that "requires persistent self-awareness, constant self-criticism, and regular self-examination" (p. 23). The mentor teacher in this chapter's opening vignette is a good example of the ongoing battle Kendi describes in his book. This teacher had reflected on the child's context and circumstances, developed a relationship with him, and adopted strategies that were perceived as effective, but wasn't aware that those practices were perpetuating inequitable opportunities for the child.

By not recognizing that the student wanted to be heard and encouraging his desire to participate, and instead rewarding what was deemed "acceptable school behavior" (staying quiet) by "allowing" him time outside the classroom, this well-meaning teacher failed to meet his real need—his need to be heard and seen within the classroom, not excluded from the classroom environment. Many diverse children, like this young boy, face challenges caused by educators' attempts to navigate the shift from racist to antiracist, as they strive to reflect on and understand the underlying causes of their students' behavior while continuing to implement disciplinary practices and policies that perpetuate inequitable consequences.

We live in a biased society that is built on systemic racism, which feeds into institutional racism that leads to inequitable school policies and practices such as grade retention, suspension, and expulsion. These policies put in place structures and barriers that intentionally boost the privileged, while holding down the rest. Children's access to, experiences in, and outcomes during and after the early years of schooling are heavily affected by the color of their skin, where they live, their home language, and their family's income bracket (Meek et al., 2020). Ongoing in-service opportunities are necessary to assist educators and administrators with the difficult task of developing the skills in self-criticism, self-examination, and self-reflection that are needed to move toward appropriate action steps that will benefit all stakeholders and counter the long-standing disparities that permeate early childhood education systems. These opportunities will help educators learn how to "cultivate a critical consciousness," in the framing of Brazilian educator and philosopher Paulo Freire, so that they can recognize and analyze systems that create and hold inequities in place (Freire, 1973).

It is insufficient to explore practices such as social-emotional learning, positive behavioral interventions and supports, or restorative practices without a racial analysis (Morris, 2022). Educators must acknowledge the barriers that are in place, such as the various institutional and instructional policies and practices that impose low expectations on racially, ethnically, and otherwise marginalized children and deny them access to the educational opportunities they deserve, suffocating their development and potential and perpetuating systemic inequities (Fritzgerald, 2020). Dedicating oneself to continuously working toward becoming an antiracist early educator is imperative in order to close the opportunity and achievement gap faced by these young students.

An antiracist early educator recognizes and acknowledges the barriers that lead to learning loss and inequitable opportunities and takes action to create equitable solutions. They understand that providing equitable opportunities to all students requires active, intentional, continuous reflection to identify and ultimately deconstruct and reconstruct the systems, policies, and practices that impact the experiences and opportunities of young children, discourage learning and development, and make schools unsafe (Meek et al., 2020).

In the case of the opening vignette, singling out the child, embarrassing him, and sending him outside to run around on the track led to him missing instructional time and, more than likely, internalizing negative messages about himself. Even if in this case it was intended as a reward, exclusion leads to dropping out (psychologically, if not physically). Punishment by exclusion or expulsion is an indicator of the "repressive socialization undercurrents rocking education's unstable bow" (Gartrell, 2023, p. 26).

Antiracist early educators are intentional, and as NAEYC (2022) states, "intentional teachers are prepared to challenge their own and others' biases that sustain systemic inequities" (p. 11). As an early educator, reflect on the following:

- An antiracist early educator understands the important role of acknowledging one's own biases and unwaveringly takes the necessary actions to actively work toward awareness by embracing the uncomfortable through listening, researching, and collaborating.
- An antiracist early educator understands that the curriculum and instructional practices should be intentionally designed based on knowledge about brain research and the multiple influences on children's development and learning, in order to eliminate barriers and instead support learning and development.
- An antiracist early educator acknowledges that the classroom environment functions as an agent of identity development and socialization and sends messages to children about who and what is valuable.
- An antiracist early educator seeks to analyze the assessments mandated by the school to ensure a strengths-based approach that focuses on assessing each child's abilities and interests to effectively support children's learning and development.
- An antiracist early educator seeks to ensure the culture and climate of the school and classroom take into account the students, their families, and their communities; appreciates the funds of knowledge each student brings to the classroom environment; and is culturally, linguistically, and ability affirming, including, celebrating, and valuing the individual voices of the children and their families.

- An antiracist early educator advocates for and young children and their families by actively engaging with them, listening to their needs, and amplifying their voices. They champion equity through advocacy and by aligning with organizations dedicated to antiracist work, helping to create systemic change.
- An antiracist early educator understands that being antiracist is an ongoing, challenging process that takes time, reflection, action, and repetition.

The ultimate question is: Are we willing to take notice, ask questions, listen, and take the action steps required to make the necessary changes to counter the detrimental effects inequitable policies and practices have on our young students? This is hard work that demands a great deal of self-reflection, self-awareness, and self-criticism.

I'll never forget the lesson I learned from Enjonae, one of my second-grade students. Typically, she was engaged in classroom activities and instruction. One day, I noticed that Enjonae had started positioning herself in the back row when we sat on the rug and was no longer participating in whole-group instruction. Additionally, she stopped completing her assignments. When I approached Enjonae and inquired about her newly observable behaviors, she immediately started to cry. She stated that I repeatedly interacted with one particular student, and she felt that she was being ignored. Although I apologized to Enjonae and explained that my intention was not to make her feel left out and that I cared about each student, it took me a full month to sufficiently demonstrate, through my actions and words, that she meant as much to me as any other student. Then, she began to participate and complete assignments again.

In this case, Enjonae used her words and her behavior to express her feelings. She taught me the valuable lesson that our young students are watching, observing, interpreting, and analyzing our every move to determine whether our actions are just, fair, and equitable. She also taught me that the decisions teachers make influence a child's reactions (emotions), which influence their behavior (attention and learning). Going back to the discussion of primary and secondary emotions (Guy-Evans,

2023), Enjonae's primary emotions were not being met, and therefore she reverted to her secondary emotions.

What we often don't realize is that our young students may not have the words to express their feelings, but instead express and communicate their emotions through behavior (Bailey, 2014). When educators do not take the time to intentionally talk to and listen to young children, the verbal expressions or signals they send are unconsciously ignored or devalued. Then, the students and their learning suffer—and often, these students, the ones who most desire a sense of safety and belonging and require our attention and patience, are the ones who are held back or face exclusionary punishments. In this way, "persistent biases against certain groups of children . . . lead to preschool push-out" (Gartrell, 2023, p. 28).

UDL: DEFINITIONS AND PRINCIPLES

NAEYC's Advancing Equity in Early Childhood Education position statement recommends that early educators do the following:

> *Acknowledge and seek to understand structural inequities and their impact over time. Take action when outcomes vary significantly by social identities (e.g., lopsided achievement test scores, number and frequency of suspensions or expulsions that disproportionately target African American and Latino boys, or engagement with certain materials and activities by gender). Look deeper at how your expectations, practices, curriculum, and/or policies may contribute (perhaps unwittingly) to inequitable outcomes for children and take steps to change them. (2019, p. 6)*

How do we accomplish this? First, antiracist early educators must take advantage of the resources and tools available to address the barriers that contribute to inequitable social, emotional, and academic opportunities. Adopting the principles of Universal Design for Learning (Rose & Meyer, 2002) as common practice ensures that decisions are based on research that supports the finding that learning is a process that occurs in three areas of the brain and that curriculum must be developmentally appropriate, be aligned to specific goals and standards, and utilize assessments that are geared toward determining how best to support students and scaffold learning (Bailey, 2014; Novak, 2016). This in turn helps to guarantee that during the early years, all children have abundant opportunities to create, explore, experiment, design, evaluate, and analyze.

In the education system today, some students are often robbed of these opportunities. Instead, their experiences are commonly shaped by a lack of developmentally appropriate practices: restricted movement, scripted curriculum, and few creative or project-based learning opportunities. As Novak (2016) states, "scripted curriculum, pacing guides, and standardized tests are barriers" (p. 16). By contrast, the UDL principles of engagement, representation, and action and expression (Rose & Meyer, 2002) ensure an inclusive approach to learning that circumvents inequities and complements the strengths of all students. Every child learns differently, has different experiences, and thus requires different learning strategies. The variability that each child brings to the classroom must be kept at the forefront of all decisions and actions, and early educators must anticipate and plan for this variability.

What Is UDL?

The UDL principles have their roots in the neuroscience of learning. David Rose and Anne Meyer (2002) identified three interrelated types of brain networks—the affective networks, the recognition networks, and the strategic networks—that guide what we learn, how we learn, and why we learn, and they mapped three key principles to these networks:

- To make best use of the affective networks, provide **multiple means of engagement**. This supports learners' motivation and resilience, stimulating interest and emotional connections to what they do in the classroom. Early educators should provide various opportunities for arousing children's attention and curiosity, accounting for diverse backgrounds, interests, and perspectives.

- To make best use of the recognition networks, provide **multiple means of representation**. This allows learners to better identify and understand information and make sense of patterns, ideas, and concepts. Early educators should support knowledge building and understanding by setting developmentally appropriate classroom expectations, welcoming questions, and providing instruction and learning opportunities in various formats and at different levels of complexity.

- To make best use of the strategic networks, provide **multiple means of action and expression**. This ensures learners can appropriately plan, execute, and monitor their actions and skills, express their new knowledge in a way that is clear to them, and understand the meaning and value of what they are learning (Novak, 2016). Early educators should offer opportunities to demonstrate understanding through a variety of formats and provide multiple options for expressing ideas, feelings, and preferences.

Using these principles, we can shape more equitable learning opportunities by considering the "who"—each child's individual contexts and intersectionalities, such as race, ethnicity, socioeconomic status, culture, gender, and more—and how these factors can impact and influence learning and learning design. An antiracist early educator must build on where the child is currently and create a strong foundation by intentionally designing the curriculum to take into account the many varied ways learners learn and the different skills, abilities, and experiences they bring to the classroom.

Consider the needs of Richard, a young student who had been diagnosed as "legally blind" at birth. His field of vision was less than 20 degrees, and he couldn't see objects more than 20 feet away clearly. While he had attended the same elementary school from prekindergarten, it wasn't until he was in an inclusive second-grade classroom that a teacher noticed he was academically behind his peers. While his social-emotional development was appropriate for his age, he was performing far below expectations in academic content areas: reading, writing, and math.

In fact, Richard was performing on a prekindergarten level in all content areas. His second-grade teacher quickly realized that they needed to intentionally and proactively partner and collaborate with the various specialists working with Richard: the occupational therapist, physical therapist, resource teacher, and speech and language pathologist. They needed to utilize one another's expertise in determining appropriate ways to adapt the curriculum and the teacher's instructional practices to meet this student's particular developmental and academic needs. Everyone involved with Richard—all key stakeholders, including his family—collaborated in planning his learning experiences, thinking explicitly about the "who," "what," "how," and "why."

Table 2-1 gives an example of the kinds of strategies Richard's teacher used to adapt the curriculum and build on his strengths, using the UDL framework to promote learning and development.

TABLE 2-1. Implementing the UDL Principles in Richard's Scenario
(Example Exercise: Identifying the Parts of a Sentence)

ENGAGEMENT	REPRESENTATION	ACTION AND EXPRESSION
The teacher engaged Richard (and all students) by using diverse materials. For example, they invited the students to co-create anchor charts on Post-it chart paper. The students worked with partners to identify specific parts of a sentence using sentence strips and were given the option to write their answers with colored markers. Afterward, the students posted their sentence strips on the labeled wall and helped the teacher identify sentence parts using Wikki Stix or highlighting tape.	Information was presented using several types of resources: for instance, by using anchor charts and Google Slides, reading a Big Book about the parts of a sentence, incorporating an Edpuzzle video discussing the parts of a sentence, and partner work.	Students were encouraged to demonstrate understanding in various ways, such as by working in pairs, using Wikki Stix and sentence strips, reenacting a part of the book, or using technology tools such as Loom, ChatterPix, or Powtoon to create a podcast or blog that discussed the parts of a sentence.

The UDL framework is appropriate for all students. While the strategies presented here were intentionally designed to meet Richard's individual abilities and needs, all students benefited from the intentional accommodations utilized by the teacher.

Teachers' perceptions of disability, and their likelihood of making special education referrals, are influenced by their professional development opportunities, available resources, child guidance strategies, and the political climate of the school—for example, whether the administration encourages or discourages such referrals (Prince & Lawrence, 1993). While Richard had an Individualized Education Program (IEP), prior to the second grade, his academic needs had not been met. His second-grade teacher understood the importance of learning about each of the identified goals within his IEP and utilizing the input of the specialists and his family to design and implement appropriate accommodations. As Morris (2022) writes, "Authentic relationships and ongoing engagements to cultivate trust with one another allow for students and educators to bring themselves to the learning process with an open mind to dismantle biases that lead to judgment or reprimand" (p. 37).

Incorporating UDL principles throughout all aspects of the early childhood curriculum is imperative to providing activities that are meaningful, relevant, and appropriately challenging for all students, regardless of their interests and abilities, and achieving the goal articulated by NAEYC (2019) that "children of all genders, with and without disabilities . . . see themselves and their families, languages, and cultures regularly and meaningfully reflected in the environment and learning materials" (p. 7). This is especially important during the early years, when young children are acquiring basic skills such as reading and writing. When the foundational skills needed for later success are not acquired during the early years, they are often harder to acquire later—in part because, too often, upper elementary, middle school, and high school teachers are trained in their specific content areas for specific age ranges, and that training might not include the early academic content skills. Thus, students who fall behind academically during the early years are likely to continue to do so, because they usually have few opportunities to catch up to their peers who are performing on grade level. The early years of a child's education are therefore crucial for overcoming barriers to learning and development.

Creating a Welcoming Environment

Research affirms the need to prioritize social-emotional development as much as cognitive and academic content-specific development, particularly for Black and Brown students (Duchesneau, 2020). A child's basic needs must be met to foster learning and development. Thus, the school and classroom environment are as important as the curriculum, instructional practices, and assessments. As NAEYC (2019) notes:

> Early childhood education settings—including centers, family childcare homes, and schools—are often among children's first communities beyond their families. These settings offer important contexts for children's learning. They should be environments in which children learn that they are valued by others, learn how to treat others with fairness and respect, and learn how to embrace human differences rather than ignore or fear them. (p. 5)

While I was teaching an early childhood classroom guidance course in Washington, DC, a graduate student who was teaching first grade brought up the challenges he was having with a student named Rebekah. He expressed his frustration at his inability to develop a relationship with her, despite multiple attempts, and shared his concern that she would likely need to repeat the year. I asked him to provide more details about her experiences and background. He explained that her parents had recently divorced and shared custody, which meant that in the middle of each week she moved houses, spending one week with one parent and the next with the other. He also mentioned that one parent was more lenient than the other. At that parent's house, she was regularly allowed to stay up until after midnight.

The two parents disagreed with each other's parenting styles, which caused constant conflict. At parent/teacher conferences, they openly contradicted each other in front of Rebekah and her teacher. My student described her as irritable and fatigued. He explained that she would often appear particularly tired at the beginning of the school week, resting her head on her desk for most of the day. During the latter part of the week, she came to school with more energy and was constantly out of her seat and engaging other students in off-task behavior. Both inattentive behaviors were frequently punished with a loss of free time or recess time.

I then asked him to reflect on the child's context, and the challenges she faced. This young girl was experiencing trauma: her parents' recent divorce, moving between two homes mid-week, lack of sufficient sleep, and quite likely stress and worry, feelings of blame and embarrassment, fear of loss of love, and various other confused and mixed emotions. As with any childhood trauma, these conditions can reasonably be expected to lead to a child feeling overwhelmed, upset, or helpless and to them acting in an atypical way, having a hard time concentrating, and showing changes in school performance (CCTASSI, n.d.).

An antiracist early educator constantly seeks to understand the multiple factors, such as home context and family dynamics, that might impact or influence each child's ability to function and learn within the school and classroom setting. It is important to remember that when a child's basic needs are not met, they may not be able to function well academically. By understanding Maslow's hierarchy of needs (discussed next) and the three types of brain networks and their role in learning, educators can determine what a child is communicating through their behavior.

Children who have experienced trauma due to various factors in their home or school environment are watching and waiting to see how long you will persist in supporting and encouraging them. As Barbara Kaiser and Judy Rasminsky (2021) note, they are looking to see if they can truly trust you. They watch you to determine and assess whether your actions match your words. Your actions, body language, and facial expressions speak louder than words. When they react to their environment, they are simply protecting themselves from the feelings associated with the trauma they have experienced: feeling hurt, unloved, unwanted, alone, afraid, and so forth. The threat triggers the "fight, flight, or freeze" mechanism, the amygdala's response to a perceived potential threat, decreasing their capacity to think about anything else. Additionally, remember the primary and secondary emotions; think about whether a child's behavior is signaling that their primary emotions were not appropriately met.

Even if you were not the initial cause of their experienced trauma, because they are in protective mode, they are testing you. Ultimately, they are waiting for you to hurt them, to disappoint them, to leave them. They want to know: How much of their behavior will you take? How long until you give up and quit? "Relationships create the brain circuits responsible for the formation of meaning, the regulation of bodily states, the modulation of emotion, and the ability to focus and sustain attention," which leads to learning (Bailey, 2014, p. 65). Particularly with students who may have experienced trauma, therefore, it is vital to take the time to form relationships in order to build the trust they need to overcome the effects of that trauma.

Maslow's Hierarchy of Needs

Overcoming trauma is a process. That process will not happen overnight. Be patient, and don't quit. Establishing trusting relationships that celebrate, embrace, and notice each child as an individual and showing that you value each child's individual differences, voice, and experiences helps make each child feel seen, respected, and valued. Said differently, an understanding of the role of trauma and of children's needs must inform curricular and instructional decisions.

Maslow's hierarchy of needs is a motivational theory of psychology developed by Abraham Maslow which states that the basic human needs can be divided into a hierarchy of five levels (McLeod, 2024). It is often depicted as a pyramid, with lower level physiological needs such as food, water, warmth, and rest at the bottom and higher level needs related to self-actualization (having a sense of purpose and meaning, creativity, inner potential, etc.) at the top. In between are our needs for safety and security, love and belonging, and self-esteem. Maslow argued that the lower level needs must be met before the higher ones can be fulfilled. Thus, if a young child's basic physiological needs are not met—if they are not fed, clothed, and rested—learning is unlikely to occur and they are unlikely to reach their full potential.

Think about the following: Why is it that if a student arrives at school late and has not eaten breakfast, if the child has missed the school breakfast window, they are often provided a snack of crackers or nothing? This means the child's basic needs are not met; they are not able to eat. Or what if, like in Rebekah's case, the child has not received the appropriate hours of sleep due to inconsistent sleep patterns because of navigating between two homes? This can cause the child to exhibit behaviors that demonstrate that they are tired and unable to concentrate. If brain research shows that three different areas of the brain—the affective, strategic, and recognition networks, responsible for the "why," the "how," and the "what"—must work together to enable learning, then why are young children punished for circumstances that are beyond their control? Put yourself in their shoes: Are you able to function optimally, pay attention, and retain information if you are hungry, if you haven't had enough sleep, or if you are experiencing a family situation that causes worry or stress?

A child's home situation is beyond their teacher's control, even if the teacher is aware of it. So what can educators do? Next in Maslow's hierarchy is the need for safety. Students need to feel safe and secure. For true learning to occur, they must trust that their school environment is safe and that they are part of a predictable and stable school and classroom community. An antiracist early educator embraces the whole child, acknowledging their strengths and areas for growth, and prioritizes decisions that favor development and learning by ensuring the school environment is a safe space and building trust and strong relationships within the classroom community. Students must feel connected to their school and their classroom community. They should know that their life inside of school is just as valued as their life outside of school.

Consider for a moment how you would describe your school's culture. Is everyone on board—the front desk staff, the custodians, every teacher? When each student walks into the building or your classroom, are they greeted by a warm smile and a welcoming comment ("Hello, I'm so glad to see you today," "Hi there, did you have a nice weekend?")? Students should be invited and encouraged to voice their concerns, needs, and wants. An antiracist early educator is attentive and eager to learn about each student to better service them. In Rebekah's case, she was experiencing trauma and upheaval at home and was attempting to communicate her need for safety and stability; reflecting more on her experiences outside the classroom better equipped my student to understand her needs in the classroom and to work to ensure they were met.

When applying Maslow's hierarchy of needs in the classroom, focusing on promoting safety and a sense of belonging can help you manage the aspects of the environment you can control, creating a foundation for students to feel secure and supported. Reflect on the following questions:

- What are my feelings about this child? Why do I feel this way? What do I know about this child's context, the many influences on the child? What actions can I take to ensure the child's basic needs are met while in the school and the classroom?

- What supports am I providing or not providing that will make it easier for this child to learn? What supports does this child need? How do I scaffold the support? Who should I involve in this process—the administrator, a social worker, the school counselor, the child's family?

Next in Maslow's hierarchy are the needs for love and belonging, esteem, and self-actualization. Intentionally providing an environment that supports a sense of belonging and connections with and between all students, where each child's voice is heard and each child is and feels respected, helps to promote social-emotional development and well-being (Rebora, 2022). Additionally, antiracist educators understand that emotion drives attention, and attention drives learning. Policies and practices that do not consider a child's basic needs contribute to the barriers that prevent development and learning.

CONCLUSION

The decisions early educators make, both overtly and unconsciously, impact young children in ways that can have lasting consequences. Policies and practices that are built on assumptions, perceptions, and beliefs that privilege some while disadvantaging others reinforce the injustices that have permeated our schools. Thus, it is imperative that curricular and instructional decisions consider a child's complete context—all of the conditions and circumstances that influence them and affect their learning—through intentional and ongoing reflection and action.

While the teacher in this chapter's opening vignette wanted to meet the child's needs and strategized to do so, his strengths were neither considered nor recognized. This young student was eager to participate and answered all the questions correctly. He exhibited advanced skills in all academic content areas. But he was bored with the content, and the expectation placed upon him that he must remain still, sitting in criss-cross applesauce for long periods, was not reasonable. Instead of challenging him academically, his teacher sent him out to the track to run as a "reward." An antiracist educator must recognize the individual strengths of each child in the classroom and adjust their practice to offer all students multiple means of engagement, representation, and action and expression—the three UDL principles.

Again, quoting NAEYC (2019):

> *With the support of the early education system as a whole, [educators] can create early learning environments that equitably distribute development and learning opportunities by helping* **all** *children experience responsive interactions that nurture their full range of social, emotional, cognitive, physical, and linguistic abilities; that reflect and model fundamental principles of fairness and justice; and that help them accomplish the goals of anti-bias education. (p. 5)*

PART II

Setting the Stage

CHAPTER 3

Creating a Welcoming Physical Environment

In anticipation of his new position as a first-grade teacher in a public school, Mr. Todd had spent many long summer nights strategically planning his physical classroom setup. He knew he wanted a space for whole-group learning, a classroom library, and a safe space area dedicated to students using resources provided to calm down and recoup if they needed a break. Also, having taught in private early care settings for three years before switching to public school, he was determined to include a dramatic play area, a science area, and a blocks/Lego area.

After a careful inspection of his classroom's layout, he quickly realized that the sleepless nights he'd devoted to planning and designing his perfect setup would need to be revised, as the space was much smaller than he had imagined. The square-shaped room would need to be divided into three main sections: a whole-group area, a table area, and a classroom library, which would double as the calming/relaxation area. Instead of dedicating specific parts of the classroom to dramatic play, science, and blocks areas, he utilized the bookshelves along the back wall. He moved the shelves, using them as dividers to section off each of the main areas within the classroom. Each set of shelves contained neatly organized and labeled baskets of materials that could be used for one of the three creative areas, encouraging exploration and discovery.

○ ○ ○

The environment where learning takes place plays an important role in promoting development and learning among young children (NAEYC, 2020). The planning of the classroom environment and the provision of relevant experiences provide opportunities for encouraging, supporting, and reinforcing learning and development (Conkbayir, 2017).

The classroom environment—the physical space where learning takes place—is a critical variable affecting student motivation, behavior, attendance, retention, and learning, and thus a vital factor in countering the preschool-to-prison pipeline. It encompasses everything from the classroom's walls, seating, and desk setup to the lunchroom, libraries, and other school spaces, as well as online learning platforms (Meyer et al., 2024). This chapter will provide an overview of the role the classroom environment plays in young children's learning and development, which is important for three key reasons:

Brain development Young children are undergoing rapid brain development, and the experiences they have impact this development.

Academic development Children spend approximately 4,000 hours in grades K–3, and their experiences within the school and classroom environment affect their short- and long-term academic development (Bullard, 2016).

Social-emotional development An inclusive classroom environment supports a sense of belonging, increases motivation, and improves focus and retention of information.

Returning to Maslow's hierarchy, all humans have certain basic physiological and psychological needs. When these basic needs are met, students can focus on learning. Children yearn for an environment that is safe, inviting, and affirming. They want a place where they can freely explore and experience new concepts and ideas, and a place where they belong. They gravitate toward and feel most comfortable in environments that incorporate and affirm their interests, identities, cultures, and abilities. Children's motivation to learn is boosted when their learning environment fosters a sense of belonging, purpose, and agency (NAEYC, 2022).

ELEMENTS OF A WELCOMING ENVIRONMENT

When I observe educators, I observe the explicit and implicit curriculum. The explicit curriculum is the plan for learning: the topics covered, materials used, and so on. The implicit curriculum includes the classroom learning environment and the atmosphere created within the classroom. When observing the implicit curriculum, I ask the following questions:

- Are there diverse pictures strategically placed on the walls?
- Are there varied types of seating options (flexible seating) available for students to choose from?
- Are students able to easily navigate the learning environment?
- Are they exhibiting excitement?
- Do they seem comfortable with the space, each other, and their teacher?
- Are all students invited to participate and made to feel part of a caring community?
- Has the classroom space been intentionally designed to promote a safe environment for learning?
- Are there opportunities for students to make choices, to explore and experiment, and to interact using various technology tools?

As part of this process, I evaluate the total physical environment: the designated learning spaces, materials available, equipment used, routines implemented, and activities presented.

When I conduct observations, I also observe the school environment beyond the classroom: the lobby, the office, the hallways, the playground, the cafeteria. These are equally important as the classroom learning environment, because the entire school community influences and impacts development and learning. A child's perception of the school and classroom environment sends them a message about who belongs, who is welcomed, which behaviors and personalities are valued, who can learn here and who cannot. Students are observant and alert, and they are aware of even the subtlest omissions.

There are three ways of evaluating a learning environment: from a physical, psychological, and social-emotional perspective. Let's look at each of these in turn.

The Physical Environment

The classroom culture and climate (the focus of the next chapter) are affected not only by the interactions and relationships within the classroom, but also by the physical characteristics and features of the learning environment. The physical environment includes aspects such as the classroom design and layout, the placement of chairs and desks or tables, the size and functionality of the space, what is displayed on the walls, and the placement of materials and resources available for each child.

Each part of the physical environment plays a role in supporting the development of meaningful relationships within the environment (National Academies of Sciences, Engineering, and Medicine, 2018). The classroom environment should be intentionally designed, as the period from birth to 5 years old is a critical time for brain development, with heightened sensitivity to environmental influences. During this period, the brain exhibits increased plasticity, meaning it has the capacity to change and adapt based on experiences (Luby et al., 2021). Early childhood education and classroom settings play a significant role in supporting this developmental process (Rakesh et al., 2024).

Ideally, a classroom should be designed and set up in a way that reduces distractions; incites creativity, exploration, and engagement; and includes spaces that promote collaboration and community-building opportunities where students can learn about and celebrate each other's individual identities, cultures, languages, and abilities. Inclusive classroom environments support accessibility and acknowledge variability among students.

Classroom Layout

While early childhood education covers ages from birth to 8 (third grade), and an infant/toddler classroom will be set up differently from a third-grade classroom, there are certain aspects that should remain consistent regardless of the age group. It is important to note that there are windows of opportunity, or important periods in brain development, where input from the environment impacts the development of motor skills, emotional control, social skills, language, and cognitive skills. According to Sousa (2022), an enriched preschool environment during the early years can help children build neural connections. Therefore, it is vital that the early childhood classroom is thoughtfully planned out and effectively implemented in a way that meets the developmental and learning needs of all students.

For instance, early childhood classrooms should include areas that promote whole-group and small-group engagement (yes, even in an infant/toddler classroom!) and interactions. These areas typically include a morning circle/closing circle area, a library area, a whole-group area, and one or more small-group areas or centers, with each one clearly defined. The whole-group area should include a large enough rug to ensure everyone in the classroom has space to join the group, if they so desire. The library area should include a rug, comfortable and inviting seating such as bean bag chairs, and diverse children's books that are rotated and changed periodically throughout the school year. The small-group areas should have relevant materials that are clearly labeled and appropriately placed at eye level for easy access, such as crayons, pencils, scissors, dry-erase boards and markers, and paints. When materials are readily accessible and well organized, students are empowered to take ownership of their classroom and learning is optimized.

When planning the layout of the classroom, teachers might need to take into consideration the overall size of the room to decide on the most important areas to include to maximize the accessibility and functionality of the space. (Think about outdoor spaces, too, and how those might be used.) For instance, to promote an inclusive classroom, ensure that students feel safe navigating the classroom and that all materials are accessible.

Develop a functional floor plan that will benefit all students. Here are some rules of thumb:

- Position students' desks so that the focal point is the front of the room.

- Ensure all desks are positioned to have visibility to the front of the room, which usually includes the SMART Board, projector, whole-group rug, calendar, schedule, and so on.
- Designate a large enough area to accommodate all students for the whole-group area.
- Consider the amount of space and proximity of students within specific areas, such as small-group areas and center time areas.
- Position the small-group areas around the perimeter of the room or the large-group area; these might include a library area, blocks area, sensory table, science exploration area, and/or dramatic play area.
- Ensure the small-group areas are positioned based on the amount of noise expected. For example, the classroom library area should not be placed next to the dramatic play area.
- Be aware of other sensory elements, such as lighting, smells, music, and the colors chosen and used.
- Position the teacher's desk in an unassuming area of the classroom, such as in a corner or at the back of the room. Remember, the teacher's role is to facilitate learning; thus, the classroom environment should be a community environment. **The focal point should not be the teacher's desk.**
- Ensure shelves are appropriately labeled and strategically placed within each center.
- Ensure the storage system is organized, uncluttered, and clearly labeled.
- Designate an area of the room that promotes self-regulation and executive function skills. This area should include items such as a soft rug or couch, mermaid pillows, timers, writing materials, books, and toys and games (playdough, fidget toys, pop-it games, etc.).

Think about the total classroom environment. Does it support an antiracist, strengths-based approach and philosophy and integrate the UDL principles by providing multiple means of engagement, representation, and action and expression? Is the classroom inviting, welcoming, and accessible for all students? Are there opportunities for students to collaborate, develop agency, and make choices? This last point is an important one—as Bailey (2014) observes:

> *The sense of powerlessness that comes from the lack of choices produces stress, shuts down the prefrontal lobes, and leaves us at the mercy of our impulses and insecurities. Not providing young children choices impedes motivation and learning efficiency is poor. When presenting specific tasks and materials to young children, it is important to provide choice because doing so releases the brain's optimal thinking chemicals, fostering confidence. (p. 202)*

Wall Space

The walls within the early childhood classroom must be responsive to the students and the families served. When teachers take the time to plan effective ways to display content created by the students, foster a sense of community and belonging, and provide opportunities for families to interact with the content displayed, children and families will feel that the environment is a safe and welcoming place.

To create a sense of community and belonging, dedicate a section of the room to pictures of the students and their families. Take care to ensure that all students and families are represented. Change the pictures throughout the school year (at least once a month), and make sure the students are able to see and interact with them. I recommend placing the display at the students' eye level so that they can refer to them throughout the day. You can extend learning by asking students to share about the pictures each time they are changed or new ones are added. Remember to think outside the box. Some families don't have access to a printer or a camera, so have a camera readily accessible to take pictures. You can also ask families to send videos of themselves and display the videos on a laptop or computer or in a digital photo frame.

Look for opportunities to display content related to children's efforts and mastery. For example, documentation walls document the process and the products of children's work. The documentation can take the form of pictures, explanations, and finished products. Remember to strategically place this content at the children's eye level as well. This encourages them to interact and engage with it and develop a sense of pride. Documentation walls can be displayed both inside and outside the classroom. Invite and encourage students to contribute content so they feel more connected to the environment. Designate a section for student celebrations. Make sure the celebration wall is placed at eye level to promote participation.

Place items such as the classroom schedule, classroom calendar, classroom jobs list, weather report, and anchor charts at eye level to encourage participation, collaboration, and engagement. Incorporate interactive instructional practices, such as placing Velcro on the back of the calendar numbers and days of the week so students can easily manipulate them, or asking students to act out the weather for the day. Clearly label and organize classroom center time areas and shelving. When possible, use real pictures of the students to label classroom-related materials. Doing so promotes representation and engagement.

Co-created anchor charts that include pictures of the students demonstrating classroom expectations should be displayed at eye level near the whole-group area. This allows these expectations to set the tone and serve as the foundation for all parts of the classroom day. When I was teaching, my favorite book to read aloud, regardless of the grade level (PK–3), was *David Goes to School* by David Shannon. I would read the book with expression and dramatization, asking probing questions and thinking aloud as I read to elicit the students' thoughts about David's actions and solicit suggestions as to what the teacher and the classroom community should have done to support his growth. When students would share a suggestion, I would ask, "Do you think we need to add that as an expectation for our classroom family?"

Flexible Seating

One strategy commonly used in early childhood classrooms is flexible seating, which allows children to choose from a variety of seating options. Flexible seating options embrace differences in preferences and ability. I recall once observing a teacher whose classroom environment was particularly inviting. The classroom library included a turquoise loveseat, U-shaped yellow bookshelves, a green bean bag chair, and two camp chairs strategically placed to promote comfort and collaboration. The classroom library included various genres of children's books, flannel board retelling characters, and anchor charts. Various seating options permitted flexibility during whole-group, small-group, and independent time. An alphabet rug was placed at the front of the classroom. In addition, there were five tables of various heights. The message I received in this classroom environment was that the teacher had designed the physical space to ensure each child had equitable access to learn in an environment tailored to their needs. The arrangement demonstrated an understanding of the variability of the students and offered flexible options for learning, development, and building social-emotional skills.

Outside Space

When outside space is available, early educators can use it to create small gardens, planting herbs, flowers, fruits, and vegetables in pots or in the ground, and perhaps start a composting bin or adopt a classroom pet. I do not have a green thumb; however, I've found that integrating the outside space, no matter the size, into the curriculum helps develop children's executive function and self-regulation skills. Many students enjoy gardening, composting, or taking care of a pet. Additionally, conducting lessons outside helps promote retention.

Taking small steps in utilizing the outside space can help to create a sense of belonging for students. It's also important to be honest with your students and their families about your goals and abilities. When I was teaching first grade, I had a composting bin and a garden. Trust me, I wasn't knowledgeable about either. I made it clear to my students and their families that I did not have a green thumb. By doing so, I modeled the importance of community building and supporting one another in development and growth; families would volunteer to lead, and I was happy to assist.

The Psychological Environment

An intentionally designed, welcoming, and safe physical environment plays a crucial role in fostering positive attitudes toward learning. It enhances students' motivation, supports academic achievement, and encourages prosocial behavior (National Center on Safe Supportive Learning Environments, n.d.). Ensuring the classroom environment is a safe, respectful, and inviting space encourages children to engage with the classroom, the curriculum, and each other. As Sousa (2022) observes, "The brain is constantly scanning its environment for stimuli to determine whether they pose a potential threat" (p. 27). Consider whether your classroom environment is set up each morning in a way that reflects the interests and needs of each child. Let them know that you are thinking about them; for example, "I noticed you seemed to enjoy reading books about dinosaurs, so I have placed a few dinosaur books in the classroom library" or "I know you love art—why don't you take a look at the new paints we just got?"

An antiracist early educator is attentive and eager to learn about each student in order to better service them and is always looking for ways to implement that knowledge within the social, temporal, and physical environment. The environment plays a crucial role in influencing how students engage with content, sustain effort, and ultimately learn (Posey, 2018). When the physical environment is thoughtfully planned and organized with each child in mind, distractions, disruptions, and delays are minimized and active learning, problem solving, and collaboration are supported and encouraged through appropriate use of space and materials. This contributes to a healthy psychological environment, where children are interested, engaged, and motivated to learn and where they feel comfortable asking questions, taking risks, and participating.

The Emotional Environment

As discussed in Chapter 2, Maslow's hierarchy of needs tells us that for students to participate fully in the learning process, their basic physiological and psychological needs, such as the need for safety and belonging, must be met. Carla Hannaford (2005) describes it as follows: "How we take in and assimilate learning is first determined by our safety, and the quality of our relationships with parents, caregivers, and siblings" (p. 16). Early childhood educators are among these caregivers.

Thus, a key aspect of the early educator's role is to build connections with all of their students, encouraging a sense of belonging for all, and to intentionally integrate the time and space for social-emotional development and well-being (Rebora, 2022). Taking into account Maslow's hierarchy of needs, understanding each child's individual context and experiences as well as how children learn is imperative to making curricular and instructional decisions. As NAEYC (2022) observes:

> *Children's behavior is impacted by a range of contributions: asynchronous development, lack of opportunity to learn and practice social skills, stress and fatigue, exposure to toxic stress, the impacts of poverty and violence, a mismatched level of challenge, the need for more or less structure or stimulation, inconsistency in routines, inadequate space and materials, the need for a different level of adult scaffolding and support, and past experiences and traumas. (p. 117)*

Trauma symptoms can manifest in several domains: physical, cognitive, social and emotional, language and communication, and learning (Institute of Education Sciences, 2023). When students feel safe, respected, scaffolded, and valued as part of the community context, learning can occur (Posey, 2018). A healthy emotional environment supports learning and the development of social-emotional and executive function skills. The classroom should be a safe space that is inviting and comfortable and provides spaces and opportunities for students to express themselves, calm down when desired, and grab a snack if warranted. For instance, I've observed classroom environments that intentionally included:

- Snack stations, including baskets filled with nut-free, allergy-free snacks and small water bottles.
- A tented "safe space," with stream lights, mermaid pillows, pictures of nature, a sound machine, and a journal station. This area also included a timer, used to demonstrate the allotted time students could spend inside the designed space.
- Calming areas with pillows, rugs, pictures of the students and their families, blankets, and snuggle items such as teddy bears. This area also included fidget toys and a timer.

It is important for the teacher to model how and when to appropriately use such spaces. For instance, during the middle of a lesson, the teacher might say, "Phew, I need time to think about how to proceed. I think I'm going to spend 2 minutes in the tent." They would then enter the tent, turn on the timer, and begin doodling in the journal. When the time was up, they would return to the group and say, "Okay. Now I've had time to breathe and think. I'm ready to proceed."

The teacher might also notice a student who might benefit from one of these spaces, and ask them whether they were hungry and needed a snack, or if they wanted to utilize the tent and whether they would like the teacher to join them inside. Teachers should take the time to repeatedly model how to appropriately and effectively use spaces like these throughout the school year, so that students know that they are available and how to use the materials within each area.

Such areas within an early childhood classroom help to make it a safe and welcoming place to develop self-regulation skills, and when students feel safe and emotionally connected to their environment, they are more likely to pay attention, participate, and behave appropriately. As Stephanie Jones and Jennifer Khan (2017) write, "Social and emotional development comprises specific skills and competencies that students need in order to set goals, manage behavior, build relationships, and process and remember information" (p. 5). This development can best occur in a supportive environment where mistakes are encouraged, attempts are expected, and successes are pathways to obtaining desired outcomes—the type of environment that is cultivated in an inclusive school and classroom community. NAEYC (2009, pp. 16–17) describes the role of the classroom community as providing a physical, emotional, and cognitive environment conducive to developing social and emotional skills and learning academic content, and lists five criteria for creating a caring classroom environment and community:

- Each member of the classroom community is valued by others.
- Relationships are recognized as vital to development and learning.
- Each member respects and is accountable to the others.

- Educators design and maintain the physical environment to protect the health and safety of the community members and to support young children's physiological needs for activity, sensory stimulation, fresh air, rest, and nourishment.
- Educators ensure members of the community feel psychologically safe.

Young children are constantly observing and reflecting upon their teachers' instructional, environmental, and assessment decisions. Their perception of whether those decisions are fair and equitable determines whether they feel they can trust the teacher and the environment. Posey (2018) states that "emotions drive how we perceive aspects of our environment, and negative emotions can taint perception, motivation, and learning" (p. 77), while the National Academies of Sciences, Engineering, and Medicine (2018) observe that "motivation to learn is fostered for learners of all ages when they perceive the school or learning environment is a place where they 'belong' and when the environment promotes their sense of agency and purpose" (p. 6). Emotionally supportive environments increase achievement, reduce school absenteeism, increase positive behavior, positively influence work habits, and improve resiliency (Mahoney et al., 2018). As Posey (2018) further comments, "When we perceive the context to be negative, that is the reality we will construct because emotions influence behavior, actions, and learning" (p. 159).

The young students we teach are still developing their social and emotional skills and learning to self-regulate their emotions, exercise self-control, and not instantly act upon them. When they perceive their environment as unfair and inequitable, they express that sentiment through their behavior (Jones & Khan, 2017). When they perceive a threat, they are likely to have an instinctive fight, flight, or freeze reaction, particularly when they do not trust the environment.

As Hammond (2014) writes, children want to "minimize social threats and maximize opportunities to connect with others in the community," and they can best do this when they feel "affirmed and included as valued members of a learning community" (p. 47). An inclusive and healthy learning environment is co-created by the school, the early educator, the students, and the families. Think about the following strategies to promote a positive social-emotional environment:

Repeatedly model appropriate self-regulation strategies and mindfulness practices.

Self-regulation is the ability to recognize and manage emotions and actions, and it is critical for learning and development (Birth To 5 Matters, n.d.). Within the last few years, more early educators have begun integrating the Conscious Discipline program (Bailey, 2014) within their classrooms. This approach intentionally designates a section of the classroom as a self-regulation/calm-down area, where students can find items such as comfortable pillows and chairs, pictures of their families, stuffed animals, fidget toys, and forms they can complete to share how they're feeling and what they need from their teacher. Similarly, integrating mindfulness practices into the early childhood learning environment "cultivates self-awareness, emotional regulation, and cognitive focus, fostering a conducive atmosphere for social-emotional development and academic readiness" (Bhandari & Douglas, 2024, p. 1).

Incorporate varied informal and formal social engagement opportunities.

Build relationships among peers by incorporating opportunities for students to engage in collaborative activities or learning tasks (in pairs, small groups, or with the whole group) where they have a shared responsibility for working collectively to achieve objectives. This approach exposes young children to multiple perspectives, shared knowledge, and active learning.

Positive classroom environments nurture a sense of belonging and safety, ultimately creating a community of engaged learners. Table 3-1 gives some examples of different aspects to consider and suggestions of resources to consult.

TABLE 3-1. Example Components and Resources for Creating a Positive Classroom Environment

COMPONENT	EXAMPLE	SUGGESTED RESOURCES
Organization of the classroom/layout	Flexible seating/space for students to play	https://blog.schoolspecialty.com/creating-an-effective-early-childhood-classroom-layout/
Materials	Culturally, linguistically, ability-appropriate materials: • High-quality, diverse children's books • Toys • Art materials • Posters • Assistive technology • Dramatic play materials (food, clothing, wigs, writing materials) Consider: • To whom is the material accessible? • Under what conditions? • For which tasks?	www.readbrightly.com https://bookcreator.com https://coloursofus.com
Opportunities for social-emotional development	Mindfulness and yoga	www.mindful.org/mindfulness-for-kids/
Opportunities for young children to have a voice	Animation tools	Blabberize (https://blabberize.com) ChatterPix Kids app Sock Puppets app

THE IMPORTANCE OF AN ONGOING REFLECTIVE PROCESS

Think about the last time you walked into a doctor's office. What did you notice about the environment? What did you notice about the employees? Now, think about the following: Were you greeted upon arrival? Were your needs met? Did you feel part of a community? Why, or why not? We all have different expectations regarding the physical layout, cleanliness, and organization of the office, the friendliness of the staff, and the attentiveness of the doctor. These expectations affect our emotions, and our emotions impact whether we will return for a follow-up appointment.

Just as our young students enter our classrooms with varying experiences, abilities, needs, and expectations, so do we, as educators. I believe we need to reflect upon the types of environments in which we feel safe and secure and have a sense of belonging as a first approach to being proactive and developing and designing inclusive spaces for our youngest learners. What's true for adults is also true for young children: "The environment we are in affects our moods, ability to form relationships, effectiveness in work or play—even our health," writes Bullard (2016, p. 3).

An inclusive early childhood classroom environment embraces an ongoing reflective process (Figure 3-1) that asks the educator to build the following:

> **Trust** Take the time to get to know each child's strengths and interests, and utilize that information to build intentional relationships with each child and their family. Model and co-create consistent expectations on how to foster a caring community within the classroom.
>
> **Positive emotions** Based on the information gathered about the children and their families, create an environment that embraces the

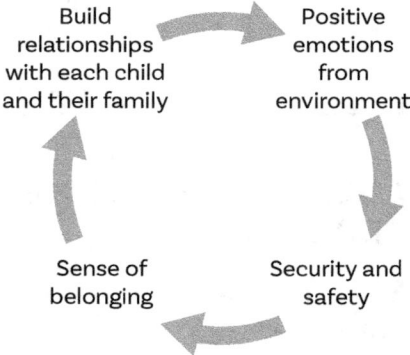

FIGURE 3-1. Creating an inclusive early childhood classroom environment is an ongoing reflective process.

strengths of each child. Children enter school with an abundance of valuable knowledge that should be utilized intentionally to build skills.

Security and safety Based on the strengths and interests of each child and their family, choose developmentally appropriate teaching materials, resources, and strategies that will help build a sense of security and safety for that student. Being well informed and observant about what is needed for each child to feel secure in the classroom space is important in the reflective process.

Sense of belonging Conduct ongoing informal assessments (discussed in Chapter 7) to ensure that each student has a sense of belonging and inclusion within the classroom environment. Utilize checklists, online journal entries, or Google Docs to collect data, and adjust the environment as needed to meet these goals. Children need to have a sense of belonging to trust, have positive emotions, and feel secure and safe in the classroom environment.

CONCLUSION

The antiracist early educator must intentionally consider the child's total environment and seek to build a classroom learning environment that fosters a sense of belonging and community. Effective early childhood school and classroom environments promote trust, safety, well-being, accessibility, and inclusivity. In an inclusive environment, curiosity, creativity, and exploration are expected and celebrated to ignite and maintain the joy of learning young children bring into the classroom. Intentional decisions are made, with input from the students and their families, about every aspect of the environment, promoting brain, academic, and social-emotional development. This includes thoughtful classroom design and layout (placement and positioning of furniture, organization of the materials, etc.), established routines, and the opportunities for relationship building. Thoughtfully and intentionally arranging the early childhood classroom in this way supports inclusion and accessibility, minimizes distractions and disruptions, and provides opportunities for collaboration and growth.

CHAPTER 4

Creating a Welcoming Culture and Climate

Ms. Sydney, a first-year kindergarten teacher, was excited to welcome her students and their families and friends to the classroom for Open House. She had prepared the classroom environment to include all the expected early childhood areas: a dramatic play area, a blocks area, a whole-group area, and center time areas.

One of the first families to join her during the Open House was Johnnie's. Johnnie was a 5-year-old who was accompanied by her grandmother. With a warm smile, Ms. Sydney welcomed the two into the classroom and invited Johnnie to explore the different classroom areas. Ms. Sydney then began engaging her grandmother in dialogue. "I'm so excited to have your granddaughter in my classroom!" she exclaimed.

Johnnie's grandmother said, "I want to tell you something. I am a 60-year-old grandmother who was granted custody of my granddaughter when she was 2 years old because her mother was unstable. Johnnie can be a handful, but please do not hesitate to call me if she becomes too much trouble."

Ms. Sydney, still excited about her first classroom, replied, "Of course I'll reach out. I know we are going to have a great school year. I've set up the classroom to ensure each child's success." Then, Ms. Sydney strolled *to the dramatic play area to join Johnnie and engage her in exploring the area and the materials it contained.*

○ ○ ○

In addition to the physical space, the classroom culture, social dynamics, and students' experiences in a learning space all contribute to the classroom environment and impact their learning. The culture and climate of the school and the classroom environment can foster hope, joy, and a curiosity for learning that extends beyond the early childhood years (Milner et al., 2019).

The culture of a school begins with the school leader. The school leader sets the policies, procedures, requirements, and expectations, which in turn shape the school's climate. The climate of the school is reflected in the organizational structures, norms, goals, values, interpersonal relationships, and teaching practices (National School Climate Council, 2009). A school's culture and climate set the tone for promoting and providing a safe environment where all members feel welcome and supported and where the physical, intellectual, and social-emotional development of all students is considered. They therefore have a large impact on children's development, learning, and achievement and on whether they and their families have a sense of belonging and trust, which leads to stronger school–family partnerships.

The school's culture is more than its mission and vision (though it should support these). It encompasses the expectations of all key stakeholders: staff, faculty, students, families, and the community. This chapter explores the role the school culture plays in promoting a positive school climate that supports development and learning and encourages reciprocal family partnerships during the early years of schooling.

A school's culture refers to the "what," "why," "when," and "where." The school's climate refers to the "how" of what is done. In other words, the school climate is an indicator of the type of school culture (Gruenert & Whitaker, 2023). School culture is important because it impacts student development and achievement, teacher effectiveness and retention, family partnerships and community support, and student enrollment

(Bohn, 2017). As Thomas Hoerr (2023) puts it, "The culture of a school communicates what is expected, which frames how every individual in the school thinks and acts."

BUILDING TRUST AND SAFETY

Relationships built on trust create a climate of respect and reassurance. These relationships are cultivated when intentional effort is made to ensure the school's culture incorporates policies, expectations, and practices that foster a sense of belonging, safety, and trust. Students (and their families) must trust that their development and learning is at the forefront of all decisions and policies. When students arrive after the late bell has rung, do we ask, "What happened? Are you OK?" Do we lead with those questions when contacting caregivers about absences or tardiness? Or do we lead with a reprimand?

When trust is established through actions, students and their families know that the school community will offer a haven of stability and provide the tools and resources needed for true learning and development. A key element of this is the purposeful development of relationships. The school leader must intentionally provide opportunities for key stakeholders within the school and the community—students, families, teachers, specialists, staff, and administrators—to connect and collaborate. An antiracist early educator seeks to understand all of their students, their families, and their communities and celebrates, appreciates, and values all of their voices. They work to create an environment where each child's comprehensive needs are assessed and accommodated. This is another important element in building a sense of trust and safety.

Families are children's first teachers. They lay the foundation for what children know and how they come to understand their identities, culture, and experiences. Just as antiracist early educators must create opportunities to include the voices of all of the children they serve, it is crucial that families are included in the school and classroom community. This means that within the school's policies and procedures, families have a voice and are thus part of shaping the school's culture.

Families want to know that they can partner with the school leader and the classroom educators, and that their voices, concerns, needs, and wants will be heard as they advocate for and support their children. In this chapter's opening vignette, Johnnie's grandmother was demonstrating this type of advocacy by speaking openly with Ms. Sydney. She proactively shared the important background information that she had been granted custody due to Johnnie's mother's instability, in hopes that the teacher would understand Johnnie's circumstances and collaborate with her if challenges arose, rather than simply viewing Johnnie with a deficit mindset.

According to NAEYC (2022), building relationships with children's families is the foundation for creating reciprocal and beneficial partnerships. Both the home and school contexts are connected to and play an important role in a child's development and learning. Therefore, it is imperative to collaborate, working together with families to further the social-emotional and academic development of young children. This type of reciprocal relationship is built on respect and trust and requires patience and reflection. Families must trust that the decisions they make for their children are respected by the school, and they must feel that the school and the educators are flexible in their approach and expectations related to engagement. We must expect variability among families. All families are different and have different expectations and different ways of being involved in their children's schooling.

A true school–family partnership embraces each family's funds of knowledge—the knowledge and skills embedded in their cultures, daily experiences, and routines—by affirming family members' contributions, collaborating on decisions, and appropriately addressing concerns, questions, needs, and challenges in a timely manner (Gerzel-Short et al., 2019; Moll et al., 1992). Drawing on these funds of knowledge through such partnerships is vital to helping young children develop in all learning domains and content areas. Furthermore, family involvement in young children's education has been linked to positive academic and behavioral outcomes (Ball, 2006). Ultimately, the school's culture should welcome all families, recognizing the varied contributions they can bring centered on the agreed-upon premise and goal of collaborative efforts to support the positive development and learning of each child.

For educators to support all of the children and families they serve, they must also evaluate and challenge their implicit and explicit biases (NAEYC, 2019). This requires careful self-reflection to identify and acknowledge conscious and unconscious beliefs and assumptions that may be affecting their interpretations of students' behaviors and their potential causes. Educators must reflect on their own cultures and norms, consider the similarities and differences between their experiences and those of their students and their families, and work collaboratively with colleagues, school leaders, families, and community leaders to explore and implement solutions. This process can help them ensure they create an inclusive and welcoming early childhood experience for all.

BARRIERS TO THE SCHOOL–FAMILY PARTNERSHIP

Too often, school policies and practices—the culture of the school—raise barriers that limit opportunities to cultivate reciprocal partnerships with diverse families. Intersectionalities such as race, class, gender, and languages spoken play a role in determining the dynamics of power, oppression, and privilege. Understanding and reflecting upon these issues is critical to advancing equitable policies and practices. Reflecting on intersectionality is vital to avoid school policies, practices, and expectations that fail to consider how cultural and linguistic differences and perspectives might be affecting school leaders' and early educators' perceptions and beliefs and their interactions and engagement with students' families.

It is important to recognize that different families have different backgrounds, cultures, and norms, which influence their experiences, expectations, and interactions with regard to engagement and building partnerships. The disconnect between home norms and school norms can create barriers that prevent positive relationships from forming. Returning to Maslow's hierarchy of needs, families have basic needs that must be met, just as schoolchildren do: shelter, food, clothing, safety, belonging. When these basic needs are not met, these factors impact family engagement and inhibit the formation of reciprocal school–family partnerships.

There are many barriers that can prevent families from developing relationships and partnerships with their children's schools, such as work schedules, lack of childcare, and lack of transportation—and these barriers in turn can lead to school leaders and educators adopting a deficit-based approach, placing blame on families and lack of parental involvement for students' behavior problems or academic failures. To avoid falling into this trap, school leaders and early educators must act intentionally, reflecting on current practices and taking the steps necessary to better understand how to partner with all families and reshape the culture of the school with their involvement. Relentlessly and continuously evaluating policies and practices that exclude, deny, and ostracize racially, ethnically, and otherwise marginalized families is the key to breaking down barriers to family engagement and partnership. Taking these necessary action steps demonstrates to students' families that they are welcomed and valued members of the school community (Gerzel-Short et al., 2019).

There are multiple considerations school leaders can take into account when developing action steps that will help dismantle the barriers diverse families are faced with at their children's schools:

- Assess the existing school policies and practices that may create barriers to effective school–family partnerships. Be alert to microaggressions—verbal and nonverbal messages that families may receive from school staff and educators about how they are perceived and valued (Sue, 2010). These can be subtle, perhaps relating to the scheduling of school events such as parent education workshops or parent/teacher conferences; consideration must be given to ensuring such events are accessible to all families.
- Involve and include all families' perspectives in the analysis and investigation of the current policies and practices. Engage families in dialogue by inviting them to share their concerns about the school's existing practices and policies and what they would like to see in revised and reimagined policies and practices.

- Co-create a revised vision and mission statement that clearly outlines action steps related to school–family partnerships by providing clear expectations for school staff and educators.

As Kamania Wynter-Hoyte and Mukkaramah Smith (2020) state, school leaders and early educators must take responsibility for providing "a more equitable, broadly knowledgeable, and anti-racist education" and building an inclusive school culture and climate that support the brilliance of young children and their families. This type of intentionality extends beyond simply creating a mission statement or adopting a vision centered on equity; it involves rethinking and overhauling current policies and practices that don't include all families but rather silence some and ostracize others. Too often, it is the privileged families who have had positive experiences with school settings that are most tuned in to their children's school culture and know how to advocate for their children. These must not be the only voices that are welcomed and heard—just as the children we support have diverse strengths and needs, so too do their families.

The school and classroom climate and environment and the daily decisions made regarding learning and development send signals to students and their families about who is and who isn't welcome. It is vital that school leaders and early educators evaluate assumptions and beliefs that can lead to misinterpretations and miscommunications and to policies and practices that leave some out while capitalizing on and valuing the assets of others, leading to missed opportunities for some children to grow. Educators must ensure that all families, like all children, have diverse ways to engage, access information, and express themselves, allowing them to become active participants in the school and classroom community. This includes providing input to the curriculum, the learning environment, and instructional and assessment practices.

Partner With Families on the Curriculum

Families need to acquire an understanding of the curriculum used within the school and classroom setting and collaborate with their children's educators and staff within the school about the best ways to disseminate content. To facilitate this, school leaders and early educators should:

- Interact regularly with families about the curriculum. Make note of the frequency, mode, content, and outcomes of those interactions so you can evaluate and improve them.
- Remain patient when providing information on curricular decisions and invite families to share feedback regarding these decisions.
- Provide multiple means of engagement, representation, and action and expression in communicating with families, per the UDL principles. For example, you might use surveys to check in with families about questions they have and their thoughts on the curriculum, use Doodle polls to set up meetings, and offer short video explanations of content and expectations.
- Provide regular explanations and opportunities to experience the curriculum. For instance, send home weekly newsletters about the curriculum in each family's preferred format: hard copy, email, text, or video.

Partner With Families on Instruction

Families also need to understand the instructional strategies used to meet the individual needs of each child in a developmentally, culturally, linguistically, and ability-appropriate way. To facilitate this, school leaders and early educators should:

- Engage families in dialogue about the hobbies, interests, and strengths of their children.
- Continuously provide varied opportunities to check in with families about their goals for their children.
- Ask engaging questions: What are you noticing? What do you suggest? How can I help? Work with the families as a team.
- Explain what you do and why. Use the UDL principles, offering multiple means of representation, engagement, and action and expression when communicating about instructional practices.

Partner With Families on the School and Classroom Environment

School leaders and early educators should work with families to co-create an inclusive school and classroom environment that embraces and celebrates differences while acknowledging similarities. To facilitate this, they should:

- Encourage family involvement in the classroom by offering various ways to engage, access information, and express themselves, such as through screencast videos, social media platforms like TikTok and Instagram, or by using QR codes that make accessing information simpler.
- Ensure the school and classroom environment is a welcoming space by adopting an open-door policy.
- Include various opportunities to appreciate and celebrate families—for example, their customs, hobbies, and occupations—within the school and classroom environment.

Partner With Families on Assessment

Explain and demonstrate to families the various assessment practices used and how to interpret the results, and make sure they understand how the results from each assessment will be used to meet the individual needs of each child. To facilitate this, school leaders and early educators should:

- Be intentional about engagement with families, keeping them informed about the types of assessments used and how data is analyzed.
- Make time to meet with families to analyze the data together and co-create relevant action steps.

Additional Ways to Promote Partnership

Here are some additional strategies to help form strong partnerships with families:

- Open a dialogue with all families. Evaluate your communication style (frequency, mode, content, outcomes) and adjust it as needed to

provide for varied means of engagement, representation, and action and expression.
- Ensure that families have access to the necessary technologies, or provide alternative ways to communicate if needed.
- Make your communications friendly, individualized, and specific.
- Minimize academic and professional jargon (e.g., avoid acronyms).
- Be responsive. Return emails, phone calls, and text messages in a timely manner (within 24–48 hours).
- Support multilingual families by providing information in the language they speak in the home and ensuring that the content is accessible and understandable. Providing important documents in multiple languages demonstrates an acceptance of and respect for diverse languages and cultures.
- Ask family members how they want to be greeted and address them accordingly.
- Create a dedicated space for families within the school. Ensure the space is welcoming for all families.
- Encourage families to share their language, culture, and family traditions with the school/student body.
- Address barriers to participating in school activities (childcare needs, transportation, etc.) by offering solutions. Engage the community to support these efforts.
- Partner with the community to offer free resources to the school, ensuring that all stakeholders have access to them.

CONCLUSION

School leaders play a pivotal role in setting and modeling the expectations that shape a school's culture and climate. Cultivating a culture built on policies and practices that foster trusting and reciprocal relationships between students, families, and key stakeholders leads to a climate where all families feel that they are heard, are seen, are valued, and belong. Intentionally and continuously evaluating the culture of the school, rethinking policies and practices that privilege some while raising barriers for others, and involving families (especially those who are most at risk) in the evaluation process ensures that all families have opportunities to use their voices and to be included and engaged in their children's learning and development.

Learning about the social, linguistic, and cultural backgrounds of the families served helps school leaders and early educators understand how best to develop relationships that form into reciprocal partnerships (Alanís et al., 2021). Respect, trust, and flexibility promote the development of these partnerships (Barron & Kinney, 2021), creating a sense of belonging for both students and their families and ensuring that the school and classroom environment feels like a safe and supporting space for everyone.

When I was a classroom teacher, our classroom community motto was "We are a family." Collectively, we would think of ways our classroom family (community) could support, encourage, respect, and celebrate one another. Each year, we would decide upon a visual signal we could use to demonstrate our connectedness as a classroom community and family. We also created a hand signal to represent our visual and our commitment to our motto. Throughout the school year, we would refer back to our visual, and we used the hand signal as a way to communicate our motto during the day. If I was absent, my students would share these with the substitute teachers and explain them. This was one way of ensuring that the classroom culture and climate were welcoming to all and conducive to development, learning, and social-emotional development.

CHAPTER 5

Creating a Welcoming Temporal Environment

Madilyn, a 4-year-old preschooler, is typically developing in the cognitive, physical, and language domains. However, she often responds to situations that cause her distress by either not speaking or crying, which her preschool teacher interprets as a refusal to engage in daily classroom activities and routines. When Madilyn exhibits these behaviors, her teacher attempts to calm her down by reading a book to her or trying to interest her in completing a puzzle or some other task, but sometimes they have to call the front office for assistance. Due to Madilyn's outbursts, her teacher has placed her in a center time group with children who are not typically developing in cognitive, physical, and language skills. During center time, the group focuses on activities like recognizing letters, gluing worksheets, and counting. However, these tasks do not support Madilyn's social-emotional development, as they don't align with her specific developmental needs. And because the pacing and content of these lessons are not developmentally appropriate for her, she frequently becomes frustrated and expresses herself by crying and refusing to work.

○ ○ ○

An antiracist early educator understands that the curriculum and instructional decisions and practices must intentionally leverage each child's strengths, skills, and background knowledge, as well as taking into account their individual interests, contexts, and experiences. The temporal environment encompasses factors like the timing, pacing, and sequencing of the curriculum and instructional practices. These elements have a significant effect on emotions, attention, learning, and development. This chapter will examine the important role the temporal environment plays in supporting social-emotional development. Additionally, we will explore the importance of incorporating active learning and the UDL principles when planning the temporal environment.

THE IMPORTANCE OF THE TEMPORAL ENVIRONMENT

As early educators, we are often expected to follow and teach from a predetermined, content-specific curriculum. In some cases, the curriculum includes expected instructional practices and materials, with predetermined standards, outcomes, and pacing guides or timelines. But this one-size-fits-all approach doesn't necessarily ensure equitable learning opportunities for all students.

In this chapter's opening vignette, Madilyn's teacher had assessed her as typically developing in all learning domains. However, because her social and emotional skills were still developing and she had difficulty using language to express and communicate her thoughts and feelings, her teacher placed her in a center time group with students who were not aligned with her cognitive skill level. But at 4 years old, isn't it "typically developing" for a young child to require guidance in expression through reflective, proactive, collaborative, and strengths-based practices and strategies? As Marjorie Fields et al. (2017) observe, children may exhibit behavior problems to avoid failure or when they do not understand their emotions and do not yet have the executive function skills to express them in a socially acceptable way.

When children exhibit behavioral concerns in the classroom, it is usually due to one of the following:

- lack of structure and routine
- lack of clarity of goals and expectations
- inappropriate pacing or timing when presenting lessons
- lack of consistency in the schedule
- lack of classroom organization
- lack of instructional supports that scaffold learning
- lack of choice, flexibility, and agency

A predictable learning environment promotes a sense of safety and security. This type of environment provides stability for all children, which is particularly important for children who exhibit behaviors such as avoidance, procrastination, self-sabotage, or outright quitting. Antiracist teachers recognize that all behavior has meaning and engage in ongoing and collaborative reflection related to all aspects of the curriculum and instructional practices, decision making, and implementation.

DESIGNING THE TEMPORAL ENVIRONMENT

As mentioned previously, the temporal environment refers to the timing, sequence, and length of routines and activities that take place throughout the school day, including transitions between them. A temporal environment that is designed intentionally and carefully supports emotional safety and ensures that the school and classroom structures and routines are implemented consistently, equitably, and predictably and that the structures that are in place are conducive to learning and development (Stafford-Brizard, 2024).

In determining routines and timing, ask yourself the following:

- Is the timing and pacing developmentally, individually, culturally, linguistically, and ability-appropriate for the age group and children you're working with?

- Are the routines developmentally appropriate and adaptable?
- Are the procedures for transitions specific and clear, and is time allowed to continuously practice those procedures?

Children learn best when our curricular decisions and instructional practices incorporate knowledge about child development and that knowledge is used to set developmentally appropriate standards and goals, implement predictable routines, and choose appropriate materials and assessments. Antiracist early educators intentionally consider and plan the temporal environment, taking into consideration both the mandates from the school and the individual and developmental needs of the students. Strengths-based school and classroom environments that encourage positive and trusting relationships release the hormone oxytocin in the brain, which helps us to bond with others through feelings of psychological safety (Kaufman, 2020).

Intentionally planning and preparing the temporal environment aids in the development of social-emotional and executive function skills. During the early years, children are still learning the rules and expectations of the school and classroom and developing these skills and their capacity for self-regulation. Executive function skills are the bridge between knowing and showing what you know, and learning environments can either create barriers to developing them or support and enhance them (Carey & Reid, 2024). Providing children with ongoing opportunities to understand the rules and expectations related to the goals, the schedule, and the routines through repeated scaffolding, modeling, and opportunities to practice sets them up for social-emotional and academic success.

Ultimately, racially, ethnically, and otherwise marginalized students are often robbed of these kinds of opportunities. Instead, the experiences and the opportunities they too readily encounter are shaped by a lack of developmentally appropriate practices and do not clearly identify and provide opportunities for mastery of the routines and expectations or the tasks and concepts presented. As Carey and Reid (2024) write: "It's not enough to offer supports for executive functions; we must teach our learners the skills and strategies to support their own executive functioning" (p. 14).

The design and implementation of school and classroom routines must tap into students' background knowledge, strengths, and needs and provide the time needed to adapt, understand, and learn new information, which requires activating neural pathways in the brain (Kaufman, 2020). Ensuring the school and classroom routines are reflective of the strengths and needs of the students served requires careful attention when planning, developing, and implementing these routines. For instance, if a teacher notices that students become lethargic or more easily agitated before lunchtime, a routine that focuses on the needs of the students and utilizes a strengths-based approach might incorporate quiet time (such as dimming the lights and conducting a yoga session) or a read aloud into the daily schedule at this time.

When thinking about routines, consider whether the expectations are clear and whether you are providing multiple means of engagement to promote access and learning. In addition, it is imperative that early childhood educators reflect upon the timing, pacing, and transitional strategies used, incorporating developmentally and individually appropriate practices. For example, brain research shows that embedding a minute or two of movement in a lesson increases retention (Sousa, 2022).

In the previous chapters, we discussed the importance of a welcoming physical environment and school culture and climate. Next, we will examine the role a welcoming and developmentally appropriate temporal environment plays in supporting learner agency, confidence, and academic success. We will explore the importance of the following aspects when designing the temporal environment:

- recognizing individual differences in development, culture, language, and ability to ensure that the temporal environment is developmentally appropriate for the students our classrooms serve
- attending to social and emotional development to build strong relationships that foster a sense of belonging and a positive identity and self-esteem, all of which are conducive to learning (Cantor et al., 2021; NAEYC, 2009)
- promoting active rather than passive learning, using all five senses to maximize positive engagement and promote retention

DESIGNING A DEVELOPMENTALLY APPROPRIATE TEMPORAL ENVIRONMENT

Attention is affected by factors such as anxiety, arousal, the difficulty of the task, interest level in the material, and the novelty and type of situation (Batshaw et al., 2019, p. 232). As Batshaw et al. observe, "The achievement of good outcomes in an educational program is dependent on the interaction between the student and teacher. Educational programs must be relevant to the child's needs and address the child's individual strengths and challenges" (pp. 258–259). This was not the case for the student described in this chapter's opening vignette, who was placed in a center time group where the activities were not suited to her developmental needs.

There are three central components in planning the temporal environment: understanding the curriculum, knowing each child's developmental and individual needs, and designing a schedule and routines that balance the expectations of the school with the needs of the students. A daily schedule that is predictable influences the classroom routines and classroom behavior. In addition, consistency is key. An early childhood classroom schedule typically includes activities like breakfast, morning meeting/circle time, small-group or center time, a read aloud, lunch, nap, recess, whole-group time, and closing circle. Maintaining a consistent sequence to this schedule each day is essential. The schedule is one of the components of the classroom environment that I look for first when I observe in early childhood classrooms. In some classrooms, the teacher reviews it every morning, just after the children enter the classroom or immediately following breakfast time. This way, if there is a change to the schedule, the teacher can alert the children at the beginning of the day.

When the temporal environment is grounded in an understanding of child development, how young children learn, and developmentally appropriate practices, the pacing and timing of the activities and lessons presented are planned appropriately. For instance, utilizing a visual timer can help with time management to monitor and manage parts of the schedule. Check out Mr. Bomb & Friends or Best Sand Timer, which can be displayed on the SMART Board for all students to see.

The temporal environment also supports the development of executive function and self-regulation skills. These skills depend on three types of brain function (Belsky, 2024):

- **working memory**, which governs our ability to retain and manipulate distinct pieces of information over short periods of time
- **mental flexibility**, which helps us to sustain or shift attention in response to different demands and to apply different rules in different settings
- **self-control**, which enables us to set priorities and resist impulsive actions or responses

Development of executive function skills is supported when children are aware of the schedule and when they know the length of time allotted for the routines and activities they will participate in throughout the day. Keep in mind that learning the expectations related to the temporal environment requires time and repetition. Students must be given opportunities to engage in activities and to practice and learn how to meet the expectations that are set for them. This is not accomplished through a predetermined, scripted curriculum that requires young children to sit, listen, recite, and complete worksheets or coloring pages. On the contrary, a positive, well-designed temporal environment supports social-emotional development through repeated opportunities for whole-group, small-group, peer, and independent interactions to develop the competencies needed to successfully navigate their classroom. Such an environment also includes opportunities for students to learn how to self-regulate through support, scaffolding, and modeling. "By creating opportunities for children to share, question, answer, collaborate, and create with one another, teachers help harness social interaction to support learning" (NAEYC, 2022, p. 96).

As discussed in Chapter 2, the affective networks of the brain correspond to the UDL principle of engagement. Anne Meyer et al. (2024) write: "Affective networks determine the emotional and motivational significance of the world around us: They motivate and prioritize what we do and what we learn" (p. 27). We can support the affective networks within the temporal environment by:

- Providing and displaying a visual schedule in a location where ALL children can see and access it.
- When using pictures to illustrate items on the schedule, incorporate photos of the actual students in the classroom.
- Referring to the schedule throughout the school day. Some teachers remove items from the schedule during the day as they are completed. I have also seen teachers use an arrow, which they move throughout the day to point to the current place in the schedule.
- Using a visual timer, like Stoplight Clock or Tico Timer, throughout the day to assist with pacing.
- Using fingerplays throughout the day to assist with implementing transitions that incorporate movement, singing, and dance.
- Being clear about goals and objectives when designing small-group instruction. For instance, consider creating math center small groups that are homogeneous, whereas small-group literacy instruction might involve heterogeneous groupings.

DESIGNING FOR SOCIAL-EMOTIONAL DEVELOPMENT

Social-emotional development includes learning to cooperate and share with others, following rules, solving problems, and self-regulating, as well as the ability to take risks and tolerate frustration when learning is difficult. According to Kostelnik et al. (2019, p. 452), there are four dimensions within the social-emotional learning domain: social skills (interacting with others), socialization (learning the values, beliefs, customs, and rules of society), social responsibility (caring for one another and our world), and social studies (learning how to contribute to the public good within a diverse and democratic society). It's important to consider each of these dimensions when planning the temporal environment.

The schedule and routines must include time and space for students to play, collaborate, and learn from one another. Fostering care and equity are two critical areas to consider when creating an environment that promotes social-emotional development and learning, as these are key characteristics of communities that support children's development and learning (NAEYC, 2022). A community cannot be said to be caring if it does not understand and give each child what they need to thrive. Equity relies on viewing each child as an individual and customizing expectations to increase access and remove barriers. Fostering care and equity involves modeling expectations, offering continuous support through time and repetition, and scaffolding both expectations and learning.

A well-organized classroom with a predictable schedule, routines, and procedures is as important as a thoughtful classroom layout for supporting social-emotional development. In a well-organized classroom, young children have varied opportunities to learn the steps, procedures, and processes to "do school," and there is ongoing and careful consideration of each child's needs. Said differently, our young children are capable of learning tasks and making choices about all things expected in the school and classroom setting when expectations are presented in developmentally appropriate ways that scaffold learning (Fields et al., 2017).

When teacher/child interactions support emotional development, children are more likely to develop key social-emotional skills such as impulse control, prosocial behavior, and social competence and are less likely to have behavior concerns. Similarly, when children understand the "why" and the "so what" of the classroom expectations and routines, they are more likely to engage in active learning activities and to develop strong social-emotional and executive function skills. Attention, information processing, and memory are accessible when the brain is in a safe state (Stafford-Brizard, 2024). Fostering social-emotional development through positive child guidance requires intentional organizational decision making and flexibility within all aspects of the classroom environment.

DESIGNING FOR ACTIVE LEARNING

NAEYC (2022) states that a comprehensive curriculum recognizes that instructional practices must integrate active learning rather than passive learning to increase the chances of maximizing positive emotions and promoting long-term memory, development, and learning. Active learning uses interactive learning methods. It recognizes that students need to move, dance, act, interact, and engage with their environment to feel as though they are part of the classroom environment. Active learning engages students in activities that utilize the five senses and extends involvement in the learning process to deepen understanding through higher order thinking—thinking on a level that is higher than memorizing facts and requires that there be multiple opportunities to understand, infer, connect, categorize, manipulate, put together, and apply knowledge (Thomas & Thorne, 2009).

By contrast, passive learning does not provide the opportunity to utilize critical thinking skills and does not typically evoke emotional connections or take into account individual student knowledge. Here are some of the characteristics of passive learning:

- The tasks require students to sit at their tables or on the rug while information is disseminated.
- The tasks are not developmentally appropriate—they may be too long, include too much detail, or be non-interactive and non-engaging.
- Curriculum and instructional practices rely on independent work and the drill and practice model. Students are required to recite information or answer predetermined questions.

In contrast, here are some of the characteristics of active learning:

- The tasks provide varied opportunities for students to set goals, produce, create, make choices, and reflect.
- The tasks incorporate learning through the use and context of games, music, movement, art, and technology tools. They promote collaboration, allow repetition, are relevant, build on the students' strengths, and are interactive, using auditory, visual, and tactile modalities.
- The timing, pacing, and activities are adaptable and accessible for all students. Students have repeated opportunities to understand the tasks and expectations.

Student engagement that evokes positive emotions helps develop the roles, responsibilities, and collaborative structures that facilitate peer interaction during tasks. This engagement also influences achievement (Pino-James, 2014). With that in mind, let's look at some ways of integrating active learning into the temporal environment.

Classroom Schedules, Routines, and Activities

When planning the classroom schedule, routines, and activities, it is important to incorporate knowledge about child development and make sure the timing and pacing are developmentally and individually appropriate. As mentioned previously, all decisions should be based on your knowledge of each of your students. Remain flexible and continuously assess or "read" the room, adjusting procedures and expectations as needed. Remember, students must have multiple opportunities and methods to engage with and demonstrate understanding of the classroom's organizational and behavioral expectations.

Here are some suggestions for integrating active learning and UDL principles when planning the timing and pacing of activities, as well as setting and communicating behavior expectations in the classroom:

Timing

To manage timing, you can:

- Use the SMART Board to display a visual timer. Remember to introduce the timer and explain the amount of time allotted for each activity, lesson, or transition. Provide time updates throughout the allotted time for each activity or part of the day.
- Use a visual GO/STOP sign to signal the start and end of an activity.
- Use music. Allow students to choose the music played during transitions, such as clean-up or line-up time.

Pacing

Incorporate knowledge about brain development and learning retention. For instance, adding a minute of movement to a lesson helps to increase oxygen and blood flow to the brain and to generate chemicals that enhance focus, motivation, memory, and mood (Sousa, 2022). Therefore, when planning the classroom schedule, routines, and activities, intentionally embed movement breaks. After years of teaching and observing in early childhood classrooms, a rule of thumb I live by is to incorporate 1 minute of movement for every 10 minutes students are expected to sit on the rug. Here are some ideas for incorporating movement:

- Play GoNoodle on the SMART Board.
- Play Simon Says.
- Use musical instruments and jam out to various types of songs.
- Play telephone.
- Use props such as scarves to dance and sing with.
- Use puppets to act out scenes, recite fingerplays, or introduce transitional activities.

Classroom expectations

The list of classroom expectations is extensive. We have guidelines for voice level, taking turns, collaborating and sharing with peers, and calming down after the minute of movement, as well as for behavior during carpet time, greeting time, and clean-up, and when walking to the rug, sitting at the table, or visiting the calm-down area, among other things. Teaching students about all of these classroom expectations requires patience and understanding of how children learn, making sure they are clear and developmentally appropriate, repeated modeling, and providing multiple opportunities to practice throughout the school day. Here are some ways you can apply active learning strategies to learning about classroom expectations:

- Allow students to act out or perform expectations.
- Conduct a talk show using a real microphone, inviting students to serve as the guests. Interview students and ask about the "why" and the "so what" for particular expectations.
- Create a TikTok video to explain procedures and expectations and play it in the classroom.

Behavior Management and Child Guidance

While behavior management in an early childhood classroom is supported by the teacher's high expectations, it's important to recognize that child guidance goes beyond that. It involves shaping behavior expectations through a range of strategies, such as modeling, teaching, fostering positive interactions, encouraging exploration, practicing active listening, and intentionally reflecting on both the classroom environment and the established expectations.

As discussed earlier, child guidance is facilitated when the classroom is well organized, expectations are clearly articulated and modeled, and students have a variety of learning opportunities. This is because students know what is expected of them and have multiple ways to engage and express themselves. When the classroom environment is productive, engaged, and active, meaningful learning will take place. Recognize that learning anything new requires cognitive energy to pay attention and determine appropriate actions to take with the new information (Posey, 2018).

Here are some ways that incorporating active learning strategies into various aspects of the temporal environment can support appropriate and effective child guidance and behavior management:

Schedule

The length of time for which young children can sit and focus varies depending on their age. For instance, for 3-year-olds, it's about 5–10 minutes; 5-year-olds can manage about 15 minutes and 7-year-olds about 25 minutes (Drinks, 2019).

Use the information on typical amounts of time for which young children can focus when planning your schedule, depending on the specific age group you are teaching. Remember to balance the schedule by incorporating active learning activities. This can help children stay engaged and focus for longer.

Routines

Present detailed steps and expectations for the various routines within the classroom, such as entering and leaving the classroom, moving between different areas in the classroom, going to the bathroom, and getting a drink of water. Include the students in establishing these routines and expectations. Also, remember to appropriately plan and communicate the steps related to and materials needed for completing specific tasks, and provide expectations about what students should do if they finish the assignment before the allotted time (for example, additional activities they can complete).

Transitions

Use transitional activities that integrate content areas in an active learning, strengths-based approach to promote productivity. Effective educators recognize that managing transitions smoothly and efficiently incorporates what we know about brain research and plays a key role in supporting social-emotional and academic development.

When I was teaching in the classroom, I created a "transitions activity necklace." I attached laminated index cards to a three-ring binder hoop. Each index card included a 2-minute transition activity that could easily be played to assist with smooth transitions. I didn't want to play the same games each week; the necklace allowed me the opportunity to quickly choose a different transitional activity each time.

Think about ways to utilize the arts within the temporal environment to promote active learning. Merryl Goldberg (2012) identifies eight principles of the role of arts in equitable education:

- The arts expand expressive outlets and provide a range of learning styles available to all children.
- The arts enable freedom of expression for second language learners.
- The arts open venues for inclusive education and reaching out to exceptional learners.
- The arts provide a stage for building self-esteem.
- The arts encourage collaboration and intergroup harmony.
- The arts empower students and teachers.

- The arts deepen teachers' awareness of children's abilities and provide alternative methods of assessment.
- The arts provide authentic cultural voices and add complexity to teaching and learning.

There are various art disciplines (dance, music, theater, visual arts) that can be implemented throughout the classroom schedule and incorporated into transitions and routines. Dance, for example, can easily be incorporated within transitions and allows students to learn through repetition, time, space, patterns, and rhythm. Music and singing also integrate concepts such as repetition and rhythm, as well as tempo and pitch. As part of the morning meeting or circle time routine, incorporate song, fingerplays, and poetry. The visual arts provide opportunities for students to express themselves and their ideas through painting, drawing, or coloring. During closing circle, students can express themselves through drawing a quick 5-minute sketch about their favorite part of the day. This is also a good activity for students who finish assignments ahead of time. Through theater and drama, such as puppetry, students have opportunities to play and use their imagination, develop language and vocabulary, and boost their social-emotional development. Teachers and students can also co-create a classroom mascot, which can be used to promote engagement during routines and transitions.

CONCLUSION

Children learn best when developmentally appropriate structures and routines are consistently and equitably implemented. By aligning these elements with our understanding of brain research and child development, we can create an environment that supports all aspects of learning and behavior. As Maslow's hierarchy of needs tells us, our young students yearn for their basic needs to be met and to trust that their environment is safe, inclusive, and responsive. The temporal environment, which includes the management of daily routines, transitions, and timing, plays a crucial role in promoting a positive classroom atmosphere. Through consistent expectations, modeling, and repeated opportunities to practice and understand the routines, it signals safety. This also helps children build social-emotional and executive function skills, enabling them to regulate their behavior.

Routines and schedules need to be clearly articulated, integrated throughout the schedule and the curriculum, and developmentally appropriate for the students to ensure that expectations are applied consistently and equitably. That said, it is also important to be somewhat flexible, recognizing that on some days the routines and methods used and the engagement and interest of the students might mean that some parts of the day last longer or end sooner than planned. For instance, the first hour might be structured as follows: welcome and greeting (5 minutes), morning message (2–5 minutes), share time (5 minutes; call on five students using equity sticks), introduction to center time (5 minutes), dismissal and time spent within the group center time areas (30–45 minutes, depending on how long the previous activities took).

It is equally important to choose, adopt, and embed developmentally appropriate transitions, timing, pacing, scheduling, and routines as it is to plan and implement appropriate curriculum and instructional practices. Trust me, I didn't leave my undergraduate program and enter my first year as a first-grade teacher ready to conquer the transition, timing, and pacing challenge! I can laugh now, reminiscing on my first year of teaching and how I expected my students to know how and where to place their backpacks and to come and sit on the rug as they entered the classroom on the first day of school. Let's just say chaos ensued the minute the morning school bell rang. I quickly learned that if the temporal environment—the schedule, routines, transitions, and procedures—was not effectively and intentionally designed, the classroom environment would not be conducive to learning and development.

PART III

Applying UDL for Inclusive, Antiracist Results

CHAPTER 6

Applying UDL to Your Planning

In a kindergarten classroom, a teacher was asked to follow a scripted literacy lesson using the book The Gingerbread Man *by Gail Yerrill. However, she recognized that the predesigned lesson didn't align with the principles of Universal Design for Learning. The original lesson involved the teacher reading the book, asking questions along the way, and using an anchor chart to teach and identify rhyming words. Drawing on her understanding of her students, brain research, and child development, the teacher decided to adapt the lesson. She introduced real gingerbread cookies as a hands-on way to connect the students with the concept of gingerbread. She asked the students if they had ever had gingerbread cookies before and, as she handed them out, encouraged each child to smell the cookie before taking a bite. This sparked a discussion about the smell and taste of the cookies. To further engage the students, she used a gingerbread man puppet throughout the story. The puppet acted out scenes and asked comprehension questions as the book progressed. Finally, the teacher incorporated an app called Edpuzzle to provide an additional way for students to express themselves and collaborate with one another, enriching their learning experience beyond the anchor chart.*

○ ○ ○

Intentionally designing, planning, and implementing curriculum and instructional practices requires an understanding of variability. Early educators should expect that there will be variability among young learners, stemming from differences in experiences, expectations, and physiology (individual differences in the affective, recognition, and strategic networks of the brain) (CAST, 2018). This means that we should expect that the students who enter our classrooms will have different needs. Isn't this the same for adults? Think about the varying strengths within your immediate family. In my case, my mother is a strong communicator and an extrovert, whereas my father is an introvert but has a passion for teaching others how to work on cars. These individual differences and strengths should be recognized, valued, and celebrated. This chapter will explore methods that take into consideration the variability young students bring into the classroom during planning and teaching.

APPLYING THE UDL GUIDELINES

Universal Design for Learning is a framework that supports teachers in removing barriers and ensuring that every young child has access to the learning environment and to the curriculum (DEC & NAEYC, 2009). A responsive and inclusive learning environment that incorporates the UDL principles is structured to create various avenues of access for young children, so that each child feels safe and comfortable taking risks, children are accepting of each other, and, ultimately, all children can thrive (Novak & Rodriguez, 2023).

Standard 4 of NAEYC's Professional Standards and Competencies for Early Childhood Educators recommends that:

> *Early childhood educators understand that teaching and learning with young children is a complex enterprise, and its details vary depending on children's ages and characteristics and on the settings in which teaching and learning occur. They (a) understand*

and demonstrate positive, caring, supportive relationships and interactions as the foundation for their work with young children. They (b) understand and use teaching skills that are responsive to the learning trajectories of young children and to the needs of each child. Early childhood educators (c) use a broad repertoire of developmentally appropriate and culturally and linguistically relevant, anti-bias, and evidence-based teaching approaches that reflect the principles of universal design for learning. (NAEYC, 2019b, p. 13)

The Division for Early Childhood of the Council for Exceptional Children (DEC) notes that "an effective curriculum framework emphasizes the interrelated and cyclical relationships between assessment, instruction, and curriculum and does not necessarily have a specific beginning or ending point" (DEC, 2007 p. 5). As this suggests, there is not one fixed, ideal way to plan and implement curriculum, instruction, and assessment practices. Rather, a universally designed classroom experience includes

- multiple means of engagement, for learning that is purposeful and reflective;
- multiple means of representation, for learning that is resourceful and authentic; and
- multiple means of action and expression, for learning that is strategic and action oriented.

The UDL Guidelines graphic organizer (Figure 6-1) is a helpful guide to assist with planning and implementation. The Guidelines provide appropriate learning supports to develop executive function skills, content-specific skills, and developmental skills throughout a lesson.

There are multiple ways to apply UDL to the various areas of the curriculum: goals/objectives, instructional methods, material selection, implementation, and assessments. Let's explore the "6 E's" approach—**encourage**, **experiences** and **exposure**, **esteem** and **empower**, and **evaluate**— within the context of the three principles of UDL.

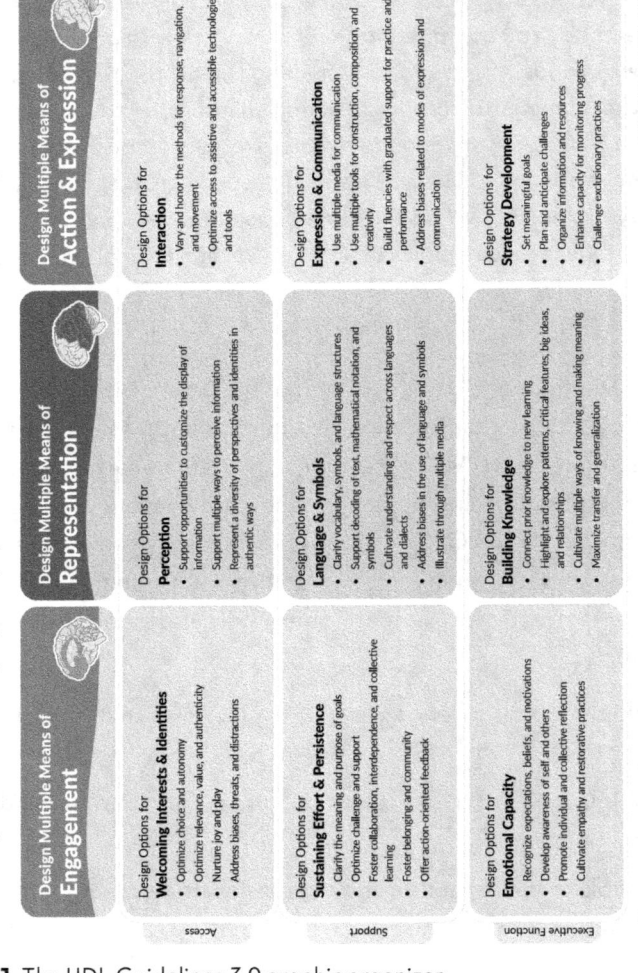

FIGURE 6-1. The UDL Guidelines 3.0 graphic organizer

Multiple Means of Engagement— Learning That Is Purposeful and Reflective

When setting goals and developing objectives, remember to consider the individual strengths and needs of each of your students. **Encourage** active engagement by incorporating technology, movement, song, art, dance, yoga, and mindfulness practices. Utilize various modalities and formats, such as whole-group, small-group, partner, and independent learning

98 Applying UDL for Inclusive, Antiracist Results

opportunities, to promote equitable opportunities to demonstrate mastery of the set goals and objectives. *For example, in a kindergarten classroom, the curriculum Fundations was mandated by the county. The teacher noticed that particular students were getting restless during the 30-minute phonics blocks as they sat in their seats reciting the letter sounds. To encourage active engagement, the teacher identified curricular and individual goals and objectives and instead conducted Fundations lessons in a circle on the rug, incorporating movement, visuals, and peer interaction. For example, students might turn to one another and use hand claps or play musical chairs while singing or chanting the letters and sounds.*

Provide vast **experiences** and opportunities for **exploration**. Bailey (2014) identifies three types of play that help promote development of self-regulation: rough-and-tumble play, dramatic play, and interactive face-to-face social play. The materials chosen and the instructional steps developed must align with the identified goals and objectives and provide varied experiences and opportunities to explore, play, and create content. *For example, a prekindergarten teacher in Northern Virginia understood the importance of an interdisciplinary approach and dedicated one center during small-group time to experimenting with and exploring different cooking activities. Students made butter, ice cream, and edible playdough while simultaneously meeting learning objectives related to math (measuring), literacy (speaking and listening), and science (experimenting).*

Build **esteem** and **empower** all students by intentionally developing positive relationships with each child and fostering a sense of belonging within the classroom. *For example, a second-grade teacher identified a student's passion for math and used his interest to connect him with peers within the classroom, to enhance social-emotional development.*

Constantly **evaluate** the goals and objectives and the instructional methods, materials, and assessments utilized in the classroom. Consider whether the formats selected allow for multiple opportunities for engagement, connection, and interaction with peers and the teacher to demonstrate understanding and mastery of the content. This type of evaluation requires an ongoing, cyclical commitment to reflection and action to promote a classroom culture and climate that support inclusion, community, learning, and development.

Multiple Means of Representation— Learning That Is Resourceful and Authentic

During the early years, young children require varied opportunities to learn and practice the "how," "why," "when," and "where" of content areas and learning domains. They are beginning to learn about themselves, who they are, their world, and how to interact with others. They are developing self-regulation, forming and developing relationships, and managing and expressing emotions as they actively explore their environment. Early educators must **encourage** them by intentionally scheduling opportunities for students to play and learn. *For example, in a third-grade classroom, students were learning about counting money. The teacher turned a section of the classroom into a grocery store, with kid-sized grocery carts and baskets, an assortment of food, two cash registers, aprons, receipts, and grocery bags. The students worked together to decide upon the prices for the groceries and who would take on the roles of customers and cashiers. This interdisciplinary approach integrated math, literacy, social studies, and social-emotional development.*

Offer **experiences** and **exploration** that extend learning and development. When thinking about goals/objectives, instructional methods, material selection, implementation, and assessments, early educators must ensure all students have equitable opportunities to obtain and grasp information. This is done by presenting content in ways that provide the time, repetition, and scaffolding needed. *For example, I have observed infant/toddler classrooms that provided varied experiences and opportunities for exploration through whole-group circle time that included singing with the young students, engaging them in conversation by asking questions, and placing the babies in a kidney table and giving them access to edible paints to promote exploration.*

Build **esteem** and **empower** students by continuously seeking ways to create a supportive and encouraging classroom community. Intentionally make time, space, and opportunities for conversation, allowing students to express themselves and learn from and with their classmates. *For example, in a toddler classroom, the teacher would engage students by providing them with choices, such as which song to sing during morning meeting.* Integrate play as a strategy to facilitate development and learning. *For example, during the years that I taught second grade, I would dedicate one corner of my classroom to a particular early childhood theme. One year, I included materials for a disc jockey: a turntable stand made out of cardboard boxes, paper and pencils, headphones, and different genres of music. Students were allowed to choose the disc jockey area during literacy centers. They could write songs or poetry, or simply listen to music on the headphones.*

Evaluate the goals set, materials chosen, information presented, and assessments conducted to ensure that they are developmentally, individually, culturally, and ability-appropriate. This should be done on an ongoing basis and requires constant reflection and action. *For example, a prekindergarten teacher recognized that one of their students was displaying particular behavior: The student was unable to retell the story during any read aloud that occurred just before lunch. After careful evaluation over the course of two weeks, the teacher devised a solution: They incorporated flannel board stories into the schedule before lunch and engaged the child by asking him to identify the sequence in the story.*

Multiple Means of Action and Expression— Learning That Is Strategic and Action Oriented

Encourage students to demonstrate that they have met goals and objectives and to show what they know and can do using a variety of instructional strategies, such as play, music, and movement. Incorporate whole-group, small-group, peer, and independent work. *For example, in a third-grade classroom, students were learning about the civil rights movement. Throughout the unit, they were encouraged to choose their preferred methods to demonstrate knowledge and understanding and allowed to decide whether to work independently, in pairs, or with a small group of peers. Students were given opportunities to conduct interviews with historians and to create videos or podcasts discussing the events and timeline of the movement. Families were invited to witness the final projects, through video and in-person presentations.*

Provide varied opportunities to **experience** and **explore** the content and individualized, scaffolded instruction and expectations. Students should have multiple options for accessing content and demonstrating understanding. Make sure to use developmentally appropriate practices—young children need time to experience and explore materials and content before learning can occur. *For example, in a first-grade classroom, students were learning about the voting process. The class acquired a pet hamster and voted on the hamster's name by participating in a mock voting poll. The teacher used Padlet, and students were each invited to create a video explaining which name they chose for the pet hamster and why.*

Build **esteem** and **empower** students by capitalizing on each child's strength and interests. Allow each student to choose the methods they would like to use to demonstrate mastery of the objectives. Recognize and appreciate the different ways they show what they know and their approaches to learning. *For instance, in a kindergarten classroom, students were allowed to choose how they wanted to complete an assignment that asked them to interview a grandparent on grandparents' day.*

Evaluate the objectives that were set, the materials that were used, and the lessons that were implemented to inform future planning and instructional steps. Use models such as the Classroom Assessment Scoring System (CLASS), a system that supports educators in focusing on improving equity, access, and impact by measuring and improving the elements of the classroom experience that matter most for supporting children's learning and development (Teachstone, n.d.). This observational instrument measures three categories or domains: emotional support, classroom organization, and instructional support. In the emotional support domain, positive climate, negative climate, teacher sensitivity, and regard for student perspectives are measured. Within the instructional support domain, concept development, quality of feedback, and language modeling are assessed to ensure high-quality, equitable instructional practices are used within the curriculum. In the classroom organization domain, behavior management, instructional learning formats, and productivity are assessed to determine how the classroom is structured. The framework focuses on answering the following questions:

- *How* can educators interact with children to best support learning?
- *How* can they use time and materials to get the most out of every moment?

- *How* can they ensure that children are engaged and stimulated?
- *How* can they ensure that *every* child has access to high-quality education? (Teachstone, n.d.)

Many school districts and early childhood programs require teachers to write lesson plans based on the curriculum. The lesson plan serves as a guide to assist with developing goals, accommodations, and strategies to meet the varying needs of the students within the classroom. Here's an example of what a lesson plan typically contains:

Lesson information Fill in the basic details of your lesson, including its title, the date it will be taught, its duration, and the intended group of students (whole-group, small-group, or one-on-one lessons).

Learning objectives Outline what students should know and be able to do by the end of the lesson. Use words from Bloom's Taxonomy to promote higher order thinking skills. *For example, "Students will be able to compare and contrast . . ."*

Standards Integrate standards from different content areas and learning domains. For example, if you are reading a children's text, does the text integrate literacy, math, social studies, social-emotional skills, and so on? If so, are you able to identify one or two long-term goals (e.g., language development, physical development, self-regulation, development of social-emotional and executive function skills) that are addressed within those content areas and/or learning domains?

Materials and resources List all the materials and digital or physical resources you'll need to effectively conduct the lesson (books, technology resources, paper, markers, glue, scissors, etc.). Keep the three UDL principles in mind when considering the resources you'll need.

Anticipatory set What strategy will you use to engage the students in the lesson? *For example, in the opening vignette, the teacher gave the students real gingerbread cookies to smell and taste and acted out scenes from the story with a puppet.* Bear in mind the primacy/recency effect—brain research tells us that the first 5 minutes and the last 5 minutes are the most memorable parts of the lesson (Watson, 2022).

UDL principles This section is at the core of the UDL lesson plan. For each UDL principle, detail how you plan to integrate equitable opportunities to demonstrate understanding of the goals:

- **Engagement:** Describe strategies to keep students motivated and engaged.
- **Representation:** Explain the varied ways you'll present content to cater to different learning preferences.
- **Action and expression:** Indicate how students will express their understanding and knowledge.

Assessment and feedback Describe how you'll evaluate students' understanding and how you'll receive and offer relevant feedback. How will you use the feedback from the students to develop action steps?

Reflection After the lesson, come back to this section. Reflect on what went well and what didn't. When were students engaged? When did students demonstrate understanding? Which parts of the lesson need reteaching, and how can that best be done? This process will help you in refining future lessons.

BE CLEAR ABOUT GOALS/OBJECTIVES

Academic and individual goals are closely linked to developmental expectations, objectives, standards, and classroom and community goals. It is essential that students and families have opportunities to understand the different type of goals to ensure clarity. Young children will need ample time to fully understand these goals and grasp their relevance to their own lives. They will also require multiple opportunities for practice, with repetition, modeling, and scaffolding strategies, to master the expected goals of the school and classroom. And always remember that before students can fully devote their attention to the curriculum, they must feel physically safe and emotionally secure in the school environment (Sousa, 2022, p. 42).

When establishing goals, think about each child's strengths and needs related to completing tasks, transitioning, and their thought patterns. Keep in mind that executive function skills—"thinking skills we use with effort and on purpose to control our behaviors and emotions and get stuff done" (Carey & Reid, 2024. p. 26)—are necessary to complete goal-directed tasks.

In the early childhood classroom, goals can be broadly classified into three categories:

Long-term goals Instructional learning goals, often set by the school's predetermined curriculum or by state-mandated standards.

Short-term goals Learning objectives that can be determined by the approved curriculum or identified by the school or teacher. These include expectations of what students should know and be able to do by the end of a lesson.

School and classroom goals These goals are typically co-created with input from various stakeholders within the community: staff, teachers, administrators, students, families, and so on.

When setting goals for their classrooms, teachers should keep these three categories in mind and consider how each type contributes to students' development across various learning domains and content areas. When planning instruction to meet the set goals and objectives, ensure that the expected outcomes are represented in ways that honor each student's intersectionalities and lived experiences. Educators should offer a variety of opportunities for children to connect with the goals and expectations, while considering their individual interests and learning preferences. Additionally, the opportunities provided to access and achieve these goals must be supported by appropriate resources, using informal assessments and ongoing reflection to measure whether students are able to demonstrate knowledge and understanding of the objectives. Remember that developmentally appropriate objectives should promote higher order thinking and executive function skills. This can be accomplished by integrating the UDL principles and the Bloom's Taxonomy framework—remembering, understanding, applying, analyzing, evaluating, and creating—into the objectives and within the instructional steps.

For example, before center time, a teacher might provide access to the instructional goals by stating the lesson's objectives in a way that sparks students' interest. In one classroom I observed, the teacher engaged the students at the start of the lesson by showing them a closed box and saying, "Today, we have four centers open. Each center will help you explore our five senses by experimenting with different items. We have four boxes. Let's open the first box to see what we're going to focus on today during centers." She then shook the box and said, "Hmm, what do you hear? What do you think is inside the box? How do you know? What other senses can we use to guess what's inside the box? Can you smell what's inside? No? What other senses can we use? Yes, we can use our sense of touch. Who would like to reach into the box—I'll open it a little—and reach inside to feel around?" Finally, the teacher asked the students to use their sense of sight to identify the box's contents. She then stated, "Now you are going to go into the centers and explore the other boxes. You'll use your senses to guess the items inside each box. There is a special box that will require you to use your sense of *taste*."

In a different kindergarten classroom, the teacher used a mystery box to engage students in learning about the fall season. They introduced the lesson by showing the students the mystery box. They then opened the box to reveal the items inside, which were related to the goals and topics for each of the center time activities: "Oh, my! I see a pumpkin. What color is this pumpkin? I see an apple. What color is this apple? I see a toy tractor. What do you think we are going to learn about this week? You're right, we are going to describe the characteristics of the season *fall* and the different types of fruits and vegetables we can harvest on the farm during the fall season." In this example, the teacher presented the goals for the center time topic ("Fall and Farm") in a developmentally appropriate and engaging way that stimulated the students' interest and participation and integrated both long-term and short-term goals.

Teachers tend to spend most of their planning time designing lessons in a way that ensures students will understand the learning objectives. However, it's equally important to remember that lessons must be relevant, offer opportunities for making connections, and be meaningful to the students (Sousa, 2022).

BE FLEXIBLE ABOUT MATERIALS AND RESOURCES USED

The materials utilized within the early childhood classroom should be developmentally, culturally, linguistically, and ability-appropriate to meet the needs of the children served. I realize that the term "materials" embodies many different items. For instance, materials can include, but are not limited to, the following:

- children's books
- art supplies
- paper
- individual easels
- flexible seating options
- different types of writing paper
- writing materials, such as pencils, pens, markers, and crayons
- dramatic play materials, such as baby dolls, grocery store materials, cash registers, money, dress-up clothes, pretend food, and a pretend refrigerator or oven
- furniture
- puppets
- stuffed animals
- blocks
- Lego bricks
- Unifix cubes
- math manipulatives
- clipboards
- scissors
- rulers
- technology tools and resources

The materials and resources used in each lesson should be chosen based on the identified goals of the lesson and centered on the needs and experiences of the students to develop executive function skills, promote relevance, and provide multiple means of engagement, representation, and action and expression. For example, if your student population may not have been exposed to coconuts, bringing in a real coconut rather than using a picture gives them that exposure and provides a rich experience that allows them to tap into their senses—touch, sight, smell, taste, hearing—and encourages long-term memory. Similarly, in the Fall and Farm lesson, displaying real pumpkins in the classroom and showing students how to carve and seed a pumpkin would help meet these goals. Taking this a step further, the dramatic play area could be transformed into a fall pumpkin patch store with materials such as real pumpkins of different sizes and shapes, a cash register, different types of apples, baskets, bales of hay, a wagon, a scarecrow, apple cider, and so on.

The materials utilized should be changed out and rotated on a regular basis to help stimulate and maintain learner interest. For instance, most early childhood classroom environments include a library area. In such an area, the children's books must be presented to the students to engage them, must include a varied representation of students' interests and lived experiences, and must be renewed and cycled on a regular basis (at least once a month). Similarly, materials within blocks, art, and dramatic play areas should be changed regularly (perhaps weekly or biweekly) based on the needs and interests of the students and to keep them engaged. Remember, the goal is to promote the development of social-emotional, executive function, and academic skills during the young years through varied experiences, broad exposure, and engagement. When students are presented with the same materials throughout the school year, boredom and disengagement ensue. Regularly changing the materials used within the classroom environment can boost engagement and motivation. Motivation enhances attention and increases the ability to process new information (Sousa, 2022).

The materials chosen for each lesson should be clearly aligned with the goals identified and the interests and needs of the students, and they should provide a variety of ways for students to demonstrate what they know and have learned.

For instance, the goals for the Fall and Farm lesson included:

- Compare and contrast the four seasons.
- Identify the characteristics of the fall season.
- Plan and act out a farm setting using the farm materials present in the blocks area.

Throughout the week, students engaged in various centers that included materials such as:

Blocks area Toy farm animals, blocks, toy tractors and trailers, toy barns

Dramatic play area Various-sized pumpkins, a cash register, farmer clothing, soil, seeds, pots, paper, pencils, books about pumpkin patches

Small-group work area Fall clothing for students to sort into piles

Technology area A virtual tour of a pumpkin patch in the local area

It is important that the materials you make available are accessible to all students in the classroom. Consider the following questions: Can the students easily locate and access the materials? Are the materials organized and clearly labeled in a way that encourages exploration, experimentation, and play, while also promoting autonomy and independence for the varied needs of the students in your classroom?

BE FLEXIBLE ABOUT INSTRUCTIONAL STEPS

The methods and/or instructional steps within each lesson must provide ongoing and diverse opportunities for young children to access the identified goals/objectives. This is accomplished by incorporating varied approaches (such as auditory, tactile, and visual learning, and independent practice as well as whole-group, small-group, and peer interactions) and by stimulating higher order thinking and executive function skills. The methods and instructional steps should also provide repeated opportunities for the teacher to check for clarity and allow for scaffolding and modeling through repetition and practice, to promote access and enable students to demonstrate their understanding of the goals.

Whoa! That sounds like a lot to consider. However, the methods and instructional steps can be viewed as a blueprint. While a blueprint serves as a plan, the plan can be changed as the teacher informally evaluates their audience, "reading the room." For instance, in the Fall and Farm example, the teacher originally placed seven items inside the box to help represent the goals and present the topic; however, after discussing the fourth item, they noticed that the students were becoming restless and starting to ask questions about the center stations.

So, the teacher closed the box and reengaged the class by saying, "Okay, I see you're excited about the centers. You should be! Let me explain each center. The first center is a farm. Who knows what we might find on a farm?" To scaffold the students' responses, the teacher then displayed the rest of the items found inside the box: farm animals, a barn, and a farmer. "You're right, we might find these items on a farm. In this center, you'll get to explore each item." By doing this, the teacher was also exhibiting knowledge about child development and developmentally appropriate practices and assessments. Too often, young children are expected to sit on the rug or in their seats and listen to instruction for longer periods of time than they are developmentally or individually capable of. When students become bored and disengaged or lose interest because of the length or difficulty of the lesson, a lack of scaffolding, or a lack of trusting relationships and a sense of belonging within the classroom community, behavior problems arise.

It is important to recruit and sustain young children's attention to promote task persistence and help them accomplish identified goals. In the previous example, the teacher's goal was to expose the students to information related to farm life during the fall season. They provided varied opportunities for exploration throughout the week during center time, but also integrated different ways for the children to demonstrate understanding of the outlined long-term and short-term goals, such as through a read aloud related to harvesting fruits and vegetables on the farm during the fall season (integrating and exposing students to rich vocabulary terms to develop content and concept knowledge), varied interactions with peers, inviting guest speakers such as a local farmer, and finally a field trip to a farm.

BE FLEXIBLE ABOUT ROUTINES

As discussed in the previous chapter, the school and classroom routines must be consistent and predictable, yet flexible. Predictability sends signals to students that this is a safe environment, which makes it easier for them to focus, engage, and take risks. However, just establishing and describing the expected routines is not sufficient for young children to accept and demonstrate mastery of them. Successful implementation of expected routines for young children requires intentional planning that includes sufficient opportunities for them to grasp the routines through repeated instruction, practice, and support.

The routines should be embedded within the schedule using varied strategies, bearing in mind that young children acquire information through attention and working memory—part of the brain's executive functions, which help the brain take in and organize new information for long-term storage. For example, many early childhood educators utilize a visual schedule to display expected routines, often incorporating pictures of the children demonstrating specific activities and parts of the day. This schedule should be continuously referenced and reviewed throughout the day. Teachers commonly refer to the schedule at the beginning of the day, during calendar time; however, to promote attention and working memory and allow them to make meaning of the information, children need repeated opportunities to hear and see the schedule.

It is also important to include children in decision making regarding the schedule and routines. This promotes collaboration and demonstrates flexibility based on the needs of the students. For instance, upon noticing that students are antsy during the math lesson, the teacher could refer to the schedule and state, "If we look at the schedule, we'll see that the next part of our day is language arts; however, what are your thoughts about taking a 5-minute recess break to increase our blood flow to the brain before returning to that lesson?"

Provide varied scaffolding and engagement strategies, and the time needed for students to demonstrate understanding of the determined goals. Depending on the curriculum used and mandates from the school or state, keep in mind that informal and formative assessment strategies should be used throughout each lesson to incite reflection on the teacher's end and inform the goals set and the instructional steps. Think about the role of a primary care doctor. The doctor has a predetermined list of questions to ask the patient; however, based on the responses from the patient, the doctor's decisions shift to meet that individual's needs. Similarly, intentional early childhood educators strategically shift their plans based on the needs of the students and "reading the room."

A few years ago, I heard the term "warm demander." A warm demander is an educator who recognizes the role their language, tone, and actions play in establishing relationships, setting goals, presenting content, promoting retention, and assessing young children, and adapts them accordingly. A warm demander is an educator who is clear and consistent, yet flexible in setting classroom routines and expectations and who integrates daily and ongoing opportunities to build community both within the classroom and with students' families. Each routine is clearly articulated, appropriately chosen, and equitably implemented, creating a sense of stability, consistency, belonging, trust, and safety. When the teacher's behavior, interactions, and communication style are welcoming and calm, and expectations are set, communicated, and scaffolded in a caring and sensitive yet firm and assertive manner, students feel safe, and this sends them the message that the teacher is supportive and fair. Children thrive and learn best in an environment free from fear, isolation, and threat. When students believe that the learning situation will lead to success, rather than them repeating past failures, both learning and development are more likely to occur.

BE CLEAR ABOUT ASSESSMENT PRACTICES (PURPOSE, PROCESS, AND RESULTS)

Provide learners with multiple opportunities to demonstrate understanding and mastery of the objectives through action and expression by ensuring they have a variety of formats for responding, demonstrating what they know, and expressing their ideas, feelings, and preferences (DEC, 2007, p. 4). The goals set, instructional practices utilized, and assessments chosen must be measurable, integrated, and interconnected. This means each one should relate to the others. In addition, each must consider the whole child and capitalize on each learner's development and strengths. Consider the various ways students obtain, retain, and demonstrate knowledge, reflect on an ongoing basis, and individualize accordingly.

As you consider the formal assessments used within your school and classroom, remember to also incorporate informal assessment strategies such as observations, checklists, and journaling throughout the year as methods to understand each child's developmental level, interests, strengths, and needs. Making sure the content is accessible to everyone will help ensure your students are engaged and able and eager to demonstrate mastery. It also promotes family involvement, as relevant discussions will permeate the classroom and extend beyond the classroom walls.

Throughout the Fall and Farm unit, for example, the teacher observed the students closely, listening to the conversations they had among themselves, taking pictures, and recording them sharing their experiences and stories related to the content. They utilized a checklist to individualize student experiences and made changes to the center areas over the course of the week to ensure students had multiple opportunities to demonstrate mastery of the goals in different ways.

Assessment—especially the formative kind that happens during instruction, when you still have an opportunity to adapt and adjust your instruction to meet learners' needs—is such an important part of the equation that it has its own chapter in this book; we'll dive more deeply into this topic in the next chapter.

IMPLEMENTATION

Over my years of teaching, researching, and coaching, I have found that there are six important steps educators should consider to intentionally implement an inclusive, strengths-based approach to curriculum and instruction:

1. Form a collaborative team.
2. Get to know the students.
3. Facilitate the lesson.
4. Observe and assess.
5. Obtain feedback on how students are building skills and habits.
6. Adjust and reteach to promote social-emotional and academic development.

Let's explore each of these in turn.

Form a Collaborative Team

Think of this step as preplanning. Preplanning requires educators to collaborate with key stakeholders (such as, but not limited to, grade-level colleagues, specialists, and/or school leaders) to ensure the curriculum and instructional practices chosen are appropriate and relevant and to expand and enhance the curriculum to integrate UDL principles. Reflect on whether the curriculum is "one-size-fits-all" and too scripted, or whether it meets the individual developmental, cultural, and linguistic needs of the students served. Remain flexible, and consistently critique and evaluate the curriculum and strategies used to determine their value in meeting the needs of the students. Katie Novak and Mike Woodlock (2021) suggest evaluating curriculum based on characteristics such as sustainability, incorporation of multiple/varied instructional activities and strategies based on student differentiation, and use of visuals, illustrations, and graphics to support multiple means of representation.

The curriculum and lesson activities should be continually evaluated and adapted with the goal of designing and implementing a strengths-based approach, taking into account the interests, abilities, and needs of each child. Educational experiences should be goal directed and designed to keep expectations high for all learners. This step requires educators to strategically use their resources and knowledge to design purposeful and intentional lessons that are accessible and flexible (Posey, n.d.-b).

Ask yourself the following questions:

- Did you collaborate with at least one other key stakeholder to ensure all plans focus on the identified goals?
- Did you incorporate relevant aspects of students' backgrounds, knowledge, experiences, and skills?
- Did you integrate UDL principles throughout lessons?
- Did you allot time to identify relevant resources and materials?

Get to Know the Students

Be prepared for variability. Integrate accommodations and differentiate to provide appropriate supports throughout each lesson. Establish relationships with your students to ensure that they have a sense of community and belonging. Recall NAEYC professional standard 4a, which states that early childhood educators should "understand and demonstrate positive, caring, supportive relationships and interactions as the foundation of [their] work with young children" (NAEYC 2019b, p. 10). This step has been emphasized throughout the book: Educators cannot teach effectively if their students do not feel safe and secure in the school and classroom environment.

As Carey and Reid (2024) observe, "UDL asks practitioners to consider the learning environment as the supporter of ability or the cause of disability" (p. 54). Said differently, the curricular and instructional decisions early educators make influence the development of young children. Intentionally integrate opportunities for students to share, discuss, and connect. Likewise, regularly assess the interactions you have with each child throughout the lesson. For example, think about the method you'll use to call on students. Will you use equity sticks (popsicle sticks used to choose volunteers to participate) or a tool like Picker Wheel? How many students will you call on at specific points throughout the lesson? If there is only enough time to call on three students, what will you say to the students who didn't have the opportunity to share but had their hands raised? How will you ensure that you follow up with those students so that their voices are heard? Integrating relationship-building activities within the classroom must become automatic rather than being an afterthought or an add-on.

Scaffold learning by giving students plenty of opportunities to engage with, learn about, and demonstrate understanding of different concepts and content areas. This can be done by incorporating activities like cooking, poetry, dancing, acting out stories, affirmations, mindfulness, and yoga into your lessons. Look for opportunities to use technology resources and hands-on materials. For example, you might have "Flashlight Friday," when you turn off the lights and students can find a space to read for 10 or 20 minutes (depending on their grade level) using their flashlights. You might also create a classroom podcast or news report: Each Monday, you can ask students to share their weekend happenings by speaking into the microphone, and throughout the week you can designate students to report on the weather, school events, and classroom learnings. Videotape or record the podcasts or news reports and share them with families, and invite families to participate in creating them.

Facilitate the Lesson

This is the fun part! Remember that the focus is on equitably facilitating engagement throughout the lesson and allowing learners to demonstrate their voice and agency. As you teach, think about the temporal environment: timing, pacing, routines, activities, and transitions. Incorporate peer interactions, recognizing that "In the process of collaborating and working with others, social/emotional skills are developed and knowledge of a topic is deepened" (Fisher & Frey, 2023, p. 80). Each part of the lesson is integral to shaping learning and development.

Keep in mind the following:

- The objectives (short-term goals) must be clear. What do you want students to know and be able to do by the end of the lesson?
- Assessments need to be ongoing and appropriately measure the objectives.
- Preplanning is vital.
- Focus on the process, rather than the outcome.
- To reduce barriers to learning, all students must have pathways to achieve the goal.
- Timing, pacing, and transitions must be developmentally and individually appropriate.
- Look for ways to embed the UDL principles within each lesson.

Observe and Assess

Assessing is an intentional, iterative process focused on continuous improvement. While it may be unrealistic to individualize summative assessments (measuring achievement at the end of a defined period or experience), this is a useful approach for formative assessments (measuring progress toward goals). Formative assessments, which may take the form of documentation, observation, checklists, and so on, are used to monitor students' understanding and permit teachers to rethink the design and implementation of lessons. They are not meant to prove that a child is exhibiting behavior problems or needs special assistance or additional outside services; rather, formative assessments, when executed appropriately, are used to adjust approaches, develop and design effective strategies, and reflect upon and manage information and resources. They offer opportunities for the teacher to focus on each child's efforts, progress, and learning strategies used and to develop strategies and action plans to use with the children and their families to ensure each child has varied opportunities to improve or grasp the concepts being presented (Sousa, 2022).

Through ongoing reflection and collaborating with a team to discuss and consider what is and what is not working, formative assessments enable educators to systemically identify acceptable, measurable, and appropriate learning outcomes and attainable goals for student learning. Understanding all children's current skills and abilities ensures access and participation and the development of appropriate learning goals, opportunities, and assessments (DEC, 2007, p. 5). Be prepared to reevaluate and adjust goals and design new strategies as needed.

Obtain Feedback

As mentioned in previous chapters, young children are constantly watching, observing, and assessing their teachers to determine whether their environment is safe, equitable, and conducive to learning. Thus, varied opportunities should be presented throughout the day for students to express themselves, ask questions, voice concerns, and share their opinions. This aligns with the UDL principle of providing multiple means of action and expression, which supports executive function skills such as setting goals and monitoring one's progress.

In addition to welcoming feedback from students, provide opportunities for students to develop individual goals and conduct-self assessments.

Yes, even preschoolers can observe, assess, and comment on their individual growth, progress, and needs as they are working toward goals, with practice and scaffolding. As early educators, we often stop ourselves from teaching students how to self-assess and provide feedback because of preconceived assumptions and low expectations due to their age, development, or other factors. However, young children are capable of this type of reflection. When teachers prioritize seeking students' input, they create inclusive classroom environments where learners are partners in building a community and are able to form the kinds of relationships with their teachers and other students that allow them to feel comfortable taking the intellectual risks necessary to learn (CASEL, n.d.).

Encourage students to:

- Discuss the learning process and how it affects them.
- Discuss their progress, what supported their learning, and where they got stuck.
- Develop a deeper understanding of what they need or don't need to achieve the goal.

Adjust and Reteach

Reflecting in order to adjust and reteach lets you consider your next instructional moves and look for additional ways to reduce barriers (Posey, n.d.-a). The reflection process encompasses the why, what, when, how, and where of teaching and allows you to ensure that all students are serviced and their needs are met, enabling them to work up to their fullest potential. The goal is to create learning opportunities that anticipate variability and plan for *all* learners. This approach changes the mindset of looking for ways to "fix" the child to one of looking at what the teacher can do differently in terms of curricular goals, assessments, instructional methods, materials, routines, and implementation.

CONCLUSION

Designing, creating, and implementing lessons that support higher order thinking and executive function and are based on developmentally appropriate and measurable objectives not only breaks down barriers to learning, but also encourages development. It nurtures students' interests, celebrates their strengths, and promotes engagement and motivation. When we design for variability using the UDL framework, we ensure that the goals and objectives we set provide varied opportunities for our students to make meaningful connections through relevant, engaging, and motivating instructional steps. This approach acknowledges that learners do not all follow a single, linear pathway in their learning. This in turn helps us to plan and proactively create learning environments that value and celebrate the uniqueness of our learners and the variability each brings to the classroom.

This process requires recognizing that systemic injustices and biases influence our curricular and instructional decisions and their implementation. We must constantly reflect, observe, and seek feedback from our students, and readjust to ensure their needs are met. This engagement and flexibility supports relationship building and encourages instructional design and implementation that lead to favorable outcomes for all students.

Our youngest learners are prewired to learn; however, many fall behind due to the lack of school experiences that capitalize on their strengths and interests and, ultimately, lack of knowledge on their teacher's part about child development, executive function skills, and how children learn. If our youngest learners lose their innate passion for learning during the early years of schooling, it is that much harder to reignite it during the later school years.

The goals, methods, and materials used are an integral part of the early childhood classroom and must be carefully considered. Children are more motivated to learn when they have opportunities to participate and collaborate and when visual, auditory, and tactile (hands-on) methods are used to support knowledge and understanding. This helps promote engagement and makes them feel connected to others, reassuring them that their environment is a safe place to learn and develop. In addition, to promote equitable access and reduce barriers to learning, the classroom environment should incorporate routines and activities that support, include, and engage children's home languages, families, and cultures.

Antiracist early educators must take advantage of the resources and tools available to address the barriers that contribute to learning loss. Providing multiple means to present information, explore content, and demonstrate understanding helps to promote positive outcomes for all learners. We must acknowledge that being different is the norm. This means there is no such thing as "normal" behavior, academic achievement, communication styles, prior knowledge and experiences, or social skills—the students who enter our schools and classrooms are far too diverse to fit in a single mold (Causton & Macleod, 2020).

○ ○ ○

Resources: CAST provides a variety of free resources and articles to support the application of UDL. Find UDL tips on developing learning goals, lesson planning considerations, and more at *https://bit.ly/UDLTips*.

CHAPTER 7

The Uses of Assessment

We are still assessing a particular student to determine the best way to support her as she has been struggling with social skills—taking turns and sharing classroom items with friends. She has been having a particularly hard time managing her emotions (tears and lying on the floor) when she does not get what she wants—the carpet spot she wanted during circle time, the toy she wanted during centers, the spot she wanted in line, the book she had to wait for while a friend finished her turn, having to put her coat on before going outside. She is also attached to a particular friend who does not always welcome this attachment. We have been assessing when the student is better able to self-regulate and at what times of the day she needs scaffolding and guidance to assist with self-regulating. We are working with her and the whole class, teaching various tools and strategies to use when they are having big feelings. I am still exploring what works and doesn't work regarding providing developmentally appropriate support in the classroom. We are awaiting a response from the child's parents to see how we can work together to best support their child at home and at school.

—Letter from a prekindergarten teacher in an urban public school setting

○ ○ ○

Assessment—both formative and summative—is an essential part of implementing the early education curriculum. An antiracist early educator understands that preconceived beliefs and biases inform and guide decisions that impact student development and learning outcomes. They also recognize that developmentally appropriate formative and summative assessments should be carefully selected, rather than relying on biased assumptions. As Alanís and Sturdivant (2023) write, "What we believe about young children and their families matters—it informs how we treat them and what they come to believe about themselves" (p. 61).

NAEYC (2022) indicates that educators must analyze the assessments mandated by their schools to ensure a strengths-based approach that focuses on assessing each child's abilities and interests and effectively supports children's learning and development. In addition, educators must be aware of, reflect on, and work against implicit and explicit biases. The information gathered must be analyzed based on what research tells us about child development, taking into account each child's individual characteristics and context (Alanís & Sturdivant, 2023, p. ix).

This chapter will highlight the role developmentally appropriate assessments play in learning about and intentionally being responsive to each child's strengths, areas of interest, experiences, family, culture, and developmental and academic needs within each of the learning domains and content areas. As Meyer et al. (2024) explain: "Assessments can become a foundation of a learning relationship. The root of the word 'assess' (the Latin *assidere*) means 'to sit beside.' This can inspire us to think about how the design of an assessment allows us to 'sit beside' a learner to understand how they are engaging with and understanding the material, relative to the learning goal that is being assessed" (p. 71).

THE ROLE OF ASSESSMENT

An antiracist educator understands the important role that ongoing developmentally, culturally, linguistically, and ability-appropriate assessments play in guiding planning, choosing appropriate supports and strategies, and collaborating with specialists and each child's family to ensure optimal development and learning (McAfee & Leong, 2015). This requires using what we know about child development and brain research to make informed and appropriate decisions about assessments that measure curricular objectives and standards and help to promote thoughtful and intentional reflection that informs instructional strategies and practices. Purposefully integrating the UDL principles within all aspects of the assessment process to promote whole-child development is essential. Technology can also be incorporated, using the SAMR (Substitution, Augmentation, Modification, and Redefinition) model to ensure it meets students' needs. Figure 7-1 summarizes these key components.

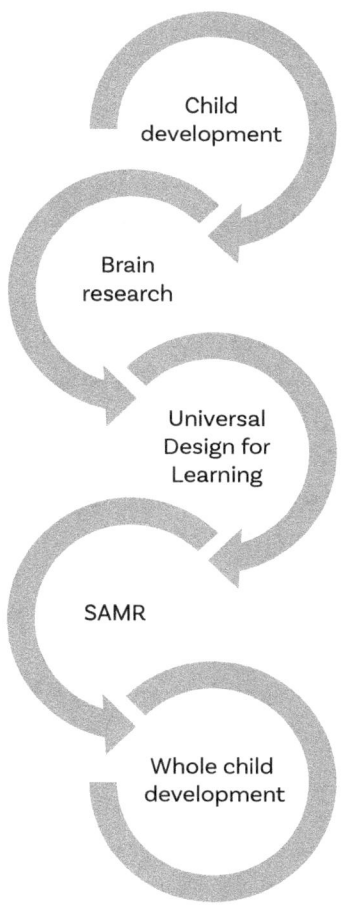

FIGURE 7-1. The cyclical process of assessing young children

To some teachers, the assessment process can seem like a daunting, time-consuming process that takes away from "more important" tasks like relationship building, routine setting, and curriculum and instructional implementation. As a new teacher, while I had graduated with a degree in education and had completed a course on assessments, I didn't immediately realize their true benefit. During my first year, I begrudgingly conducted the required summative assessments and painstakingly shared the information with my students' families during parent/teacher conferences. It wasn't until my second year of teaching that I realized the data I was collecting on each child could be used to inform my instruction and the implementation strategies I chose, and that this would have a positive impact on my students' learning and development. It was as if a light bulb went off! Once I had this epiphany, I began to understand the true value of conducting both formative and summative assessments. I came to realize that assessment was a continuous, cyclical process of gathering information and reflecting on it to determine whether set goals have been accomplished and whether the appropriate individualized scaffolds are provided.

Ongoing, developmentally appropriate assessments measure what children know, what they understand, what they can apply, and what they need to know (Odhiambo et al., 2015, p. 225). The assessment process thus involves three steps: gathering information, documenting, and reflecting on the information (NAEYC, 2022). Its primary goal is to understand children's learning and development strengths and needs in order to determine the supports required to assist with progress. Multiple types of assessments should be used to make decisions about each child, and assessment practices should include all stakeholders: the child, family, teachers, and other related service personnel, such as occupational therapists, school counselors, and speech and language pathologists (Mindes & Jung, 2015).

Our students will have a range of social-emotional, cognitive, and physical needs and abilities, and they rely on us to support and enhance their development. We need to meet them where they are. Consider the case of Natalia, an 8-year-old third grader who enjoyed the social aspect of school but, according to her language arts teacher, displayed a lack of focus and preferred engaging other students around her in conversation to completing her assigned tasks. Reflecting on Natalia's tendency to talk in class, the teacher decided to give her a personal index card with a reminder of the language arts class's expectations written on it to keep on her desk. The card read: "Sit in your seat. Face the teacher. Write your name on your paper. Raise your hand. Finish your work before getting out of your seat."

Natalia had a different teacher for math, and he expressed no concerns about her behavior. He made sure she sat in the front of the classroom during math time. He noticed that she was fully engaged when he used visuals and manipulatives. He also observed that Natalia was more engaged when he used authentic assessments that had real-world application and required self-direction and problem solving.

The way the two teachers described their observations was telling. The language arts teacher wrote: "Natalia wasn't focused and tended to stare into space daydreaming during instructional time." Her descriptions of this student were subjective, reflecting her personal assumptions and biases. The language arts teacher had singled Natalia out. She was the only student with an index card on her desk. Furthermore, when this teacher's strategies did not regain Natalia's engagement, her one-size-fits-all assessment approach led her to assume that Natalia had a cognitive processing disorder and needed additional services. Natalia was expected to behave, perform, and retain the information presented in the exact same way as the other students in her class, in the time allotted. This approach did not give Natalia the opportunity to demonstrate her knowledge, understanding, or skills in an authentic way (Novak, 2016).

By contrast, the math teacher wrote an objective, anecdotal assessment of Natalia. He described her as a child who sits at the front of the classroom during math instructional time. "When provided with visuals and math manipulatives," he wrote, "Natalia raises her hand to participate. She collaborates with peers to solve the problems and asks for help when she needs help." Natalia's math teacher assessed her to determine her strengths and interests and used that information to inform his instructional practices. He created relevant and meaningful opportunities for engagement, representation, and action and expression using choice, projects, and peer interactions. He appropriately assessed Natalia and implemented instructional practices and strategies that were supportive and encouraging, that provided multiple opportunities for Natalia to demonstrate content understanding, and that didn't single her out but included her and ensured she felt she belonged.

TYPES OF FORMATIVE AND SUMMATIVE ASSESSMENTS

A variety of assessments, both formative and summative, must be used to develop a comprehensive understanding of each child's strengths, interests, growth, and needs. Educators should carefully document their observations and the insights gained through the assessment process. They must then reflect on this information, considering how it applies to each learning domain and content area, and use it to identify the necessary supports to facilitate each child's learning and development.

Formative assessments help educators understand what children can do at the moment, identify emerging skills to support, and guide instructional planning. They also provide valuable opportunities to reflect on what's working and what's not (NAEYC, 2022). This type of assessment often involves children and their families, focusing more on the process than the final product (NAEYC, 2020). Formative assessments are conducted throughout the school year and can include documentation boards, informal observations, checklists for individual learning domains, anecdotal notes, and interest inventories.

Summative assessments are conducted at specific points, typically at the end of an instructional period or lesson, to determine if students have achieved the expected outcomes, milestones, and developmental trajectories. These assessments focus more on the final product, with the primary goal being to measure learning and information retention (NAEYC, 2020). Examples include rubrics, standardized tests, quizzes, and final projects.

As Mindes and Jung (2015) note, "informed observation requires knowledge of child development and expected learning outcomes" (p. 3). Teachers must understand when, why, what, and how to assess and should incorporate a combination of developmentally appropriate formative and summative assessments to analyze and determine each child's strengths and needs within each of the learning domains and content areas.

There are a vast number of technology resources that educators can use to aid in conducting formative and summative assessments. For example, tools like ChatterPix, Padlet, Goosechase, and Sock Puppets can be used to assess young children's knowledge and understanding of identified goals and outcomes. We'll talk more about incorporating technology as a way to accommodate learners' needs, inform instruction, and integrate varied opportunities for engagement, representation, and action and expression in Chapter 9.

BARRIERS THAT PREVENT APPROPRIATE ASSESSMENT PRACTICES

Educators face many potential barriers when conducting assessments. Inadequate knowledge about the purpose and proper implementation of different types of assessments and how to analyze and apply the results is a common problem. Too often, early educators face barriers that prevent them from learning about the intended goals of assessments, their role in the assessment process, appropriately conducting assessments, and using the results of assessments to make decisions.

One of the main barriers is lack of adequate time to effectively interpret the state standards, understand the expectations of the curriculum, and determine how to effectively use the information derived from the assessments to discern whether they have been met. Standards and developmental learning objectives provide typical expectations of specific knowledge and skills for particular age groups and grades. While educators understand that these set expectations are desired end goals, due to time constraints and additional obligations, administrators and teachers often do not have the time they need to thoroughly evaluate the standards, work out what their students need to know or be able to do, and determine how best to assess whether the standards have been met (Novak, 2016). This is detrimental to the students who need the most guidance and support and can serve as a barrier to learning for students, who are more likely to start school on an unequal footing due to disparities in school readiness (García & Weiss, 2015).

Likewise, the lack of adequate training and time impedes the most basic benefit of assessments: to use the data to inform instructional and environmental decisions. Students who are not appropriately assessed risk being assessed as academically behind or recommended for special education. This is because of interpretations of assessments that are often biased and neglect to account for the social, cultural, and linguistic skills and experiences young children of color bring to the school and classroom environment (Dobbins et al., 2016). For instance, I once observed a teacher conducting an assessment where the student was instructed to identify the object in a picture. The picture was of a snail. The student said, "Circle." Perhaps this young child had never seen a snail?

Racially, ethnically, and otherwise marginalized students are more likely to encounter teaching and assessment practices that undermine the knowledge and experiences they bring to the classroom, rather than treating them as assets. This can lead to these students being silenced, misbehaving, or withdrawing from school, and to students either being held back or being pushed to the next grade without the basic foundational skills needed to succeed in a higher grade.

Another potential barrier is lack of knowledge about the Individualized Education Program (IEP) process, how to effectively assist students with disabilities with Section 504 plans, and how to work productively with the special education staff (we will cover these topics further in Chapter 8). Insufficient time to work as a team with relevant specialists and special education staff also serves as a barrier to the appropriate use of assessments.

Collectively, these barriers can lead to early educators adopting a deficit rather than a strengths-based approach. A deficit approach focuses on identifying perceived weaknesses rather than highlighting an individual child's strengths, interests, and talents in order to promote engagement, representation, and action and expression. For example, in Natalia's case, the language arts teacher saw her talkativeness as a problem and determined that the best way to assist Natalia was to provide her with an index card inked with reminders about how she was expected to behave. This strategy did not capitalize on Natalia's assets, but instead singled her out in the classroom because she was the only student with such a card.

In a deficit approach, assessments are used to identify areas where a child is not meeting goals and expectations and where improvement is perceived to be needed. This approach communicates to the child that they are failing to or not able to accomplish the specified task. Rather than supporting whole-child learning and development, it focuses on problems and what is lacking. In contrast, the early educator in this chapter's opening vignette used a strengths-based approach to informally assess the student and reflect on appropriate instructional practices that capitalized on her strengths while simultaneously addressing her needs.

A deficit approach in assessments tends to lead to the same mindset in decision making about classroom environment practices, curriculum, and instructional methods, and it can perpetuate exclusion and bias. NAEYC (2022) outlines four steps to minimizing the effects of implicit biases on the assessment process:

- recognizing how one's own culture can affect expectations for children, the way children are assessed, and the judgments made based on assessment results
- focusing on documenting children's strengths rather than looking for ways they may demonstrate deficits or not meet expectations
- using multiple assessment strategies, including anecdotal observations and informal assessment tools so that children have multiple ways to demonstrate their competencies
- paying careful attention to whether the assessment tool has been shown to be reliable and valid for use with children who have similar characteristics to the children being assessed

NAEYC (2022) also suggests being cautious when selecting assessments, interpreting results, and deciding on intervention programs and strategies. So how do you ensure that you are taking a strengths-based rather than a deficit-based approach to using assessment information to inform your instruction and practices?

EMBRACING THE STRENGTHS-BASED APPROACH

A strengths-based approach acknowledges that the process of collecting and documenting data from assessments of each child is an ongoing, iterative process (Figure 7-2). It recognizes that the assessment process encompasses learning what each child can do and identifying their strengths, hobbies, and interests by building relationships with the children and their families; setting individually and developmentally appropriate goals for each learning domain and content area; and utilizing the UDL principles to identify appropriate and effective instructional practices and implementation strategies. In an antiracist, strengths-based approach, assessment data and results help determine areas for growth to inform curricular, instructional, and environmental decisions. Developmentally appropriate strengths-based assessments allow teachers to assess student learning in response to specific standards or developmental outcomes to determine what each student can express and allow them to demonstrate and apply what they have learned (Novak, 2016).

Authentic, informal assessments are used to get to know each child, set goals, choose appropriate instructional strategies and practices, and determine whether the goals are met. As Janet Alleman and Jere Brophy

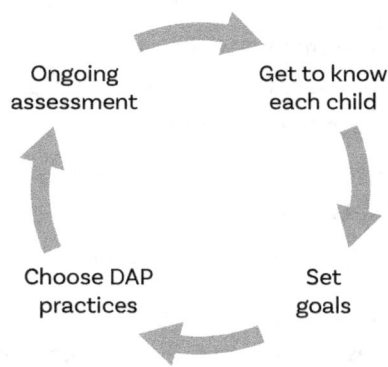

FIGURE 7-2. Assessment is cyclical.

(1999) state, "Assessment should be woven throughout the instructional units and instructional steps, formulated around the content standards, and used . . . to monitor, adjust, revise, and expand what is taught" (p. 2). When educators embed assessments throughout all stages of learning—prior to presenting the new content, at suitable junctures thereafter, and after the lesson is completed—students have multiple opportunities to demonstrate mastery, and teachers have multiple opportunities to adapt and reteach.

The pre-assessments, conducted before the lesson begins to determine what students already know, help the teacher determine whether the goals and purpose of the lesson are appropriate or need to be adjusted. Ongoing assessments, conducted throughout the lesson, assist the teacher in continuously evaluating to determine which students are mastering the objectives and which students need additional scaffolding. Finally, the post-assessments revolve around determining whether all students were able to master the objectives and providing additional support and reteaching as needed.

Assessments are therefore a critical part of teaching, as they demonstrate what students already know about the content we are presenting, what knowledge they acquire throughout the lessons, and how effective the lessons are at meeting the identified objectives. This in turn allows us to determine if and how our instructional practices should be altered to ensure all students are able to access and make sense of the content and gain the knowledge we are seeking to impart (Seefeldt et al., 2013).

Throughout this process, applying the UDL principles acknowledges that the students we serve are diverse with diverse experiences and abilities, and that it is essential to utilize various types of assessments and instructional strategies to accommodate the variability students bring to the classroom.

Some questions to ask yourself include:

- How do the selected assessment options align with the goal? That is, what is the desired outcome that students need to demonstrate, related to what they know, can do, or understand?
- Are the assessments authentic and relevant?
- What ongoing opportunities are provided to gain feedback and assess progress toward the goal?

INTEGRATING KNOWLEDGE ABOUT CHILD DEVELOPMENT

An understanding of child development and developmental milestones—skills most young children acquire during specific time frames—is essential to interpreting assessments and individualizing instruction in a way that promotes equitable learning opportunities. Early childhood educators should familiarize themselves with what constitutes typical development for their students' ages within each of the learning domains: language, social and emotional, physical, cognitive, and gross motor. Understanding the full range of what is considered typical development helps reduce the barriers to appropriately assessing and evaluating young students. A useful tool for familiarizing oneself with typical developmental expectations is the Ages and Stages Questionnaires (ASQ). A free version is available at https://agesandstages.com/free-resources/asq-calculator/.

The most important factor to consider when assessing a child is their age, including both years and months. Including the months helps to determine whether the child is on the younger end, in the middle, or on the older end of the typical development range for their age group.

Consider this example: When my daughter was 3 years old, the school leader approached me one afternoon at pickup to inform me that they were recommending occupational and physical therapy for her. When I inquired about what assessments had been conducted that led to this recommendation, the school leader told me she had been observed falling out of her chair in the classroom. When I asked how many times this had happened, she said just once in the month since school had started. However, it is developmentally appropriate for 3-year-olds to fall out of their chairs occasionally, as they are still developing small and gross motor skills at that age. Additionally, my daughter's birthday is at the end of May. Therefore, at the beginning of the school year in August, she was 3 years and 3 months old, on the younger side of the age range in her preschool class. Research on child development tells us that the window of opportunity for motor development is from the prenatal period to approximately age 5 (Gabbard, 1998). This means that she still had plenty of time to develop her motor skills, with support and experience.

Remember, developmentally appropriate practices and assessments take into account typical development, individual development, as well as culture, linguistic, and ability factors. Incorporating knowledge about child development along with an understanding of each student's lived experiences helps ensure content and assessments are relevant and meaningful to the learner.

THE 5 E'S RELATED TO ASSESSMENT AND UNIVERSAL DESIGN FOR LEARNING

As discussed previously, knowledge of child development, typical development, and brain research is imperative for educators in order to choose appropriate assessments to inform how best to meet the developmental and learning needs of each child. As Sousa (2022) explains, emotions affect memory processing, and for students to be able to learn, they must feel physically safe and emotionally secure. Further, what a child learns is most likely to get stored in long-term memory if it makes sense to them and has meaning. Knowledge about child development and brain research has led me to identify my own set of 5 E's (similar to the 5 E instructional model, and not to be confused with the 6 E's discussed in the previous chapter) as the key ingredients needed to intentionally, purposefully, and effectively integrate informal and ongoing assessments within the early childhood classroom: **experience**, **engagement**, **exploration**, **expectations**, and **evaluation**.

Experience

Knowledge is gained through experiences and exposure, not by focusing on individual deficits. The experiences educators provide in the classroom signal to young students our commitment to meeting their developmental and learning needs. While we often recognize the importance of curriculum and instructional experiences, we may overlook how these experiences can also serve as valuable opportunities for informal assessment.

When assessing young children, remember to provide multiple means of representation and experiences tailored to different sensory preferences and learning styles. Propose hands-on/tactile activities; for example, create a calm-down area where students have access to therapy playdough, fidget toys, timers, and art supplies. Incorporate technology, using the SAMR model to ensure it provides opportunities for modification and redefinition. Model and scaffold all expectations, and expect to repeat, repeat, repeat.

Engagement and Exploration

Our brains need time and repeated exposure to new content to determine whether the information presented to us makes sense and has meaning (Sousa, 2022).

When assessing young children, remember to provide multiple means of engagement throughout the assessment process and to allow for repeated exploration over a long period, to give students varied opportunities to demonstrate understanding and mastery. Incorporate everyday activities: cooking, taking a walk, listening to music, playing games, field trips.

Expectations

Set high expectations and hold students accountable for new learning. Avoid misinterpreting behaviors and data outcomes as intentional. Remember, emotions enhance retention (Sousa, 2022).

Here are a few suggestions to consider while conducting and analyzing data from assessments:

- Set expectations collaboratively with students and adjust and clarify as needed.
- Remain flexible and individualize expectations.
- Hold students accountable for their own learning and evaluation.
- Provide time for young children to explore, make predictions, observe, reflect, and come to conclusions through choice.
- Provide ongoing feedback and scaffold accordingly.

Evaluate

Finally, work with your team to evaluate the data obtained from the varied assessments. The team should include the child, their family, relevant specialists, grade-level colleagues, the school counselor, and so on. When discussing the data obtained, remember to use strengths-based, objective language rather than a deficit approach (subjective). Avoid mislabeling the child or their abilities.

Here are a few suggestions to consider allowing for multiple means of action and expression:

- Remember that the assessment process is ongoing. Repeat the process, adapting instructional strategies and practices as needed.
- Work with your team.
- Remain flexible. Teach, repeat, teach, assess, make changes, provide choice and opportunities, and repeat.

Remember that curriculum, instruction, and assessment are interrelated. The curriculum is what is taught, the instruction is how the curriculum is taught, and the assessments chosen measure whether the objectives and standards set have been met.

Here are some things to keep in mind in conducting ongoing assessments:

- Assess and reflect on which engaging strategies are working, when they work, and how they work with each child.
- Consider whether any accommodations, such as assistive technology or augmentative communication techniques, will help engage the child and promote learning.
- Partner with each student's family. Ensure that there are multiple opportunities for families to learn about the mandated standards/goals and assessments. Make sure the school and classroom environment is a safe space for families where they have a sense of belonging. Provide opportunities for them to share their goals for their children, and collaborate with them and make sure they understand how goals are developed and assessed.
- Incorporate documentation boards. Take pictures throughout the day. At the end of the day or week, arrange the pictures on a wall in the classroom or hallway and provide brief explanations related

to the curricular themes and instructional activities, incorporating the children's and their families' voices. Documentation boards can also include QR codes for easy access to additional information and pictures and/or videos of the students.

- Create assessment notes for each child. Each day, observe:
  - level of participation
  - time of day
  - frequency of occurrence
  - additional needs

These notes can also be sent home each day or at the end of the week as a way to communicate with families and share the child's strengths with them.

When planning instruction in the early childhood years, it's crucial to incorporate knowledge of brain research and child development, identify long-term goals (standards), and conduct both informal and formal assessments to guide the next steps and future lessons. Additionally, lesson planning must be developmentally appropriate, taking into account timing, pacing, expectations, objectives, instructional steps, and assessments.

CONCLUSION

The early childhood education field is a demanding one. Early educators are faced with daily decisions and requirements and expectations from the administration, the school district, students, and their families. Conducting mandated assessments is just one piece of the puzzle in ensuring that these requirements and expectations are met. There are many factors that impact early educators' beliefs about and interpretations of the assessment processes used within school systems. However, appropriate assessment practices that are developmentally appropriate and strengths based are invaluable for supporting and guiding the decisions made for each individual child and ensuring the best possible outcomes. Intentional, carefully considered use of formative and summative assessments can inform goal setting and instructional practices and strategies, thus reducing the barriers and inequities many diverse students face in early education that could have lasting, long-term effects on their development and learning and their life trajectories.

When young children experience a lack of success, are misidentified with learning difficulties or behavioral challenges, and do not receive appropriate educational services in the early grades, this can lead to feelings of discouragement and alienation from school (Allen & Cowdery, 2015; York, 2016). Utilizing a strengths-based approach within the assessment process ensures that educators intentionally assess each child's strengths, interests, and abilities. In addition, educators must continuously reflect upon their biases and beliefs, ensure appropriate assessments are used for each child, and choose tailored, engaging strategies and resources based on the observations and results. This approach will help to promote achievement for all students, in all learning domains and academic content areas.

Appropriate assessments recognize variability among students, and the data obtained from formative and summative assessments can be used to support learning and development. Antiracist educators integrate varied assessment strategies and practices within all aspects of the classroom to promote and foster growth and development.

CHAPTER 8

The Role of the Individualized Education Program

Dear Ms. Smith,

Thank you for meeting with me to discuss my son's behavior and progress thus far. I want to follow up with this email to share strategies that we are using for him in our home that are proving to be successful.

We have established a clear set of goals, expectations, and routine for our son. When our son wakes up, he knows his routine because we have it written on a chalkboard in his bedroom, but we also have modeled and supported him. We expect that you will establish a routine and engage him in instruction that will promote social, emotional, and academic confidence and self-esteem. Because, at our home, we know he has positive self-esteem and self-confidence.

There are times when we have noticed our son become shy and timid and withdrawn in the school setting. He has questioned whether he is liked by his teachers, peers, and school leaders because he is constantly sent to the principal's office. Our son responds well to supportive, encouraging, engaging, trusting adults who take the time to develop predictable, emotionally supportive, and reliable relationships with him. However, our son does not respond well to punitive, unpredictable, negative engagements that are escalated by adults. In these settings, he becomes scared, timid, and reserved.

Yes, he is six years old and in the first grade, but we have expectations for him and for you, his teachers. Thank you for taking the time to read this email and to see my child as the capable, smart, and loving child that he is.

Warmly, Jonathan's mother

○ ○ ○

The DEC's Early Interventionist/Early Childhood Special Educator (EI/ECSE) Standards recommend that "in partnership with families and other professionals, [educators] develop and implement individualized plans" and that they "analyze, interpret, document, and share assessment information using a strengths-based approach with families and other professionals for eligibility determination, outcome/goal development, planning instruction and intervention, monitoring progress, and reporting" (DEC, 2020, p. 1).

As introduced in Chapter 1, the Individuals with Disabilities Education Act (IDEA) is a federal special education law that guarantees a free appropriate public education and the provision of special education and related services to eligible children with disabilities (USDOE, n.d.-b). It defines special education as "specially designed instruction, at no cost to the parents, to meet the unique needs of a child with a disability" (Sec. 300.39.a.1).

Infants and toddlers (birth through age 2) with disabilities and their families are eligible to receive early intervention services under IDEA Part C, including the development of an Individualized Family Service Plan, or IFSP. An IFSP is a written document that outlines the early intervention services and supports a child and their family will receive, and the expected results or outcomes (USDOE, 2017). Children ages 3 through 21 are eligible to receive special education and related services under IDEA Part B.

Bateman and Cline (2016) describe four main characteristics of special education: it is *individualized*, it may include *modifications* of teaching practices and strategies, its services are systemically *monitored*, and its recipients also receive any *related services* they require to ensure an appropriate education, such as transportation, speech pathology, audiology, physical therapy, occupational therapy, therapeutic recreation, social work, medical services, counseling, and recreational services (pp. 12–13).

An Individualized Education Program, or IEP, is developed for each child attending public school who requires special education. An IEP is a legal document or plan that maps out the program of special instruction, supports, goals, and services a particular child needs to make progress in school. It is a contract between the school and the parents, outlining the services that will be provided and laying out measurable objectives tailored to the individual student's needs. This chapter will examine the IEP process and the role of the early educator in that process. We will also explore additional supports that are available, such as Section 504 plans, behavior support plans, and other relevant resources.

THE IEP TEAM

The IEP team consists of the child's parents and/or other persons knowledgeable about the child (e.g., guardian or caregiver), the child's general education teacher, the school's special education teacher(s), school psychologists or counselors, specialists who can interpret evaluation results or data (speech language pathologists, occupational therapists, physical therapists, audiologists, etc.), and a school district representative or school leader who has the power to approve school resources for the child. The goal of the team is to plan the individual student's special education experience at the school. They meet regularly (at least once a year) and work collaboratively to evaluate the student's needs, set achievable, measurable goals, and identify the services and supports to put in place to enable the student to meet those objectives.

While the early educator is always part of a child's IEP team, often the goals and strategies discussed during the IEP meeting are implemented by the primary specialist. The school administrator is responsible for ensuring that all required resources are available and monitoring the implementation of the agreed-upon program and the student's progress. However, the support and involvement of the entire team is necessary to make sure the IEP is implemented as intended and to maximize the likelihood of the student meeting the defined objectives. This means that all members of the IEP team—family members, administrators, school counselors, specialists, early educators, instructional assistants, and paraprofessionals—must fully understand, agree on, and have a voice in the decision making related to the identified goals and the strategies to ensure the goals are accomplished and to support the child in effectively demonstrating what they know or can do.

A key requirement of IDEA is that students with disabilities should be educated with their chronologically aged peers in the least restrictive environment possible—generally, in general education classrooms with appropriate supports and services to meet their individualized needs and goals. Therefore, it is crucial that art, music, physical education, and any other specialists who work with students with IEPs understand effective strategies for supporting each child.

THE EARLY EDUCATOR'S ROLE IN DEVELOPING AN IEP

Early educators play a vital role in the IEP process. This is because they are typically the first ones to recognize a child's need, and they must then assess that need, help determine whether additional supports are required, and advocate for those supports. Upon recognizing that a child is exhibiting learning or behavior difficulties, many early educators will attempt specific strategies to address their needs before referring the student for a formal evaluation and beginning the IEP process. These strategies could relate to making changes to the classroom environment or adjusting academic or behavioral instructional methods, delivery options, and assessment practices.

If the teacher determines that the strategies they have put in place are not having the desired effect, they may refer the child for evaluation for special education services. If the evaluation results indicate that the student is eligible for these services, the IEP process will begin. The steps and changes implemented by the teacher will be presented to the IEP team, who will examine and consider the student's identified needs and current levels of performance. This will inform the development and implementation of the IEP. The annual goals and short-term objectives are determined during the IEP meeting, based on the child's present performance. Special requirements and considerations are also determined and identified; the IEP should state any accommodations that are needed with regard to presentation and responding (how students receive information and demonstrate what they know), scheduling (timing, pacing, breaks), and the classroom setting (seating, lighting, small-group or individual instruction, etc.) and any modifications that change what a student is taught or expected to learn (Bateman & Cline, 2016, p. 75). The frequency and duration of services, method and time frame for monitoring progress and communicating progress to the student's family, and placement of services (where the student will receive special education services) will also be discussed during the IEP meeting.

Differences Between an IEP and a 504 Plan

The Rehabilitation Act of 1973 (PL 93-112) was the U.S.'s first civil rights law for people with disabilities. Section 504 of this act is a national law that protects qualified individuals from discrimination based on disability. It states that "no otherwise qualified individual with a disability in the United States . . . shall solely by reason of her or his disability, be excluded from the participation in, be denied the benefits of, or be subjected to discrimination under any program or activity receiving Federal financial assistance" (USDOE, n.d.-a). Recipients of this assistance include public school districts and other state and local education agencies. Section 504 thus protects any student attending a school that receives federal financial aid who has a record of or is regarded as having a disability, defined as a physical or mental impairment that substantially limits one or more major life activities, including learning (USDOE, n.d.-a).

In contrast, to qualify for an IEP, a child must meet the requirements for at least one of the 13 categories of disability recognized by IDEA as impacting children's schooling: autism, deaf-blindness, deafness, emotional disturbance, hearing impairment, intellectual disability, multiple disabilities, orthopedic impairment, other health impairment (including ADHD), specific learning disability, speech or language impairment, traumatic brain injury, or visual impairment (USDOE, 2018). Therefore, a student who does not qualify for an IEP might still qualify for a Section 504 plan. Typical qualifying conditions for a section 504 plan include (Bateman & Cline, 2016, p. 84):

- ADD/ADHD
- AIDS/HIV
- allergies
- arthritis
- cancer
- cerebral palsy
- conduct disorders
- depression
- diabetes
- eating disorders
- epilepsy
- heart disease
- hemophilia
- past drug/alcohol addiction
- temporary conditions (such as broken limbs) due to accident or illness
- Tourette syndrome
- visual impairment

Section 504 requires a school district to provide a free appropriate public education to any qualifying student in that district's jurisdiction, regardless of the nature or severity of their disability. It further stipulates that students with disabilities must be provided appropriate supports and services designed to meet their individual educational needs as adequately as the needs of students without disabilities are met. Students with Section 504 plans are usually taught in regular classrooms and do not necessarily receive supplementary or special education services.

Determining whether a student qualifies as disabled under Section 504 requires going through an evaluation process to ensure they are not misclassified, unnecessarily labeled as having a disability, or incorrectly placed (USDOE, n.d.-a). The tests used "must be selected and administered so as best to ensure that the test results accurately reflect the student's aptitude or achievement or other factor being measured rather than reflect the student's disability"; the tests and other evaluation materials must also be administered by trained personnel and validated for the specific purpose for which they are used (USDOE, n.d.-a). The information obtained from all sources as part of the evaluation—aptitude and achievement tests, teacher recommendations, evaluations of physical condition, and so on—must be documented, and factors related to the student's learning process (social and cultural background, adaptive behaviors, etc.) must be considered.

Generally speaking, the general education teacher, school leader/administrator, school counselor, school nurse, and special education teacher should be involved in the 504 process, although the members of the team who develop the 504 plan differ from state to state. The student's family is usually involved in the process, but unlike with the IEP process, this is not mandatory. Also unlike with the IEP, there are fewer requirements for what the plan must contain and fewer guarantees about implementation, monitoring, and reporting of results (Understood, n.d.). The 504 plan identifies the specific aids, services, and accommodations a student is expected to receive and the parties responsible for providing them. It may also involve modifications to what a student is taught or expected to learn. It's important to note that the general education teacher should work collaboratively with the rest of the team to implement the provisions of the plan.

Table 8-1 summarizes the some of the main similarities and differences between an IEP and a Section 504 plan.

TABLE 8-1. Comparison of an IEP and a 504 Plan

	DEFINITION	TEAM	EVALUATION STRUCTURE
IEP	A formal, written plan that details the special education services and supports a school will provide to meet the needs of student with a disability, who will provide the services, for how much time each week, and where. All required accommodations and modifications are listed. The IEP also lays out specific, measurable goals, the method and frequency of progress monitoring, and the method of communicating progress.	Parents or caregivers General education teacher Special education teacher Specialists School counselor District representative/administrator	The plan is reviewed at least once a year, and the student must be reevaluated at least once every three years. The IEP includes an evaluation of the child's current capabilities and skill levels and specifies annual and short-term objectives. Progress is monitored and reported throughout the year.

(continued)

TABLE 8-1. Comparison of an IEP and a 504 Plan (*continued*)

	DEFINITION	TEAM	EVALUATION STRUCTURE
504	A formal plan for how a school will remove barriers so a student with a disability can learn alongside peers in a general education setting. The plan does not have to be written. It generally outlines any accommodations (changes to the student's learning environment) that will be made and assistive technology or tools the school will provide, and names the person responsible for implementing the plan.	Parents or caregivers General education teacher Special education teacher School administrator/leader School counselor School nurse	The plan is reviewed at least once a year, and the student must be reevaluated at least once every three years.

What Should Teachers Know?

The general education teacher is a key part of the team when a student has an IEP, a 504 plan, or both. It is vital that they familiarize themselves with the IEP and/or 504 process and plan, the IEP goals and 504 provisions, the timeline, and the various members of the team who will be involved in implementing the plan. Teachers may need to incorporate assistive technologies like computer software, visual aids, or mobility equipment in the classroom. The IEP may also specify accommodations such as extra time for testing, oral instructions, or recorded lessons. It is essential for the teacher to ensure the classroom environment aligns with the IEP's provisions.

It is also vital that the teacher collaborate with the whole team to work collectively toward the identified goals and support the student's growth and progress. I learned the importance of this relatively early in my teaching career. After a few years as a general education teacher, I realized that while I was invited to IEP meetings to share observations and provide feedback, I was never invited to collaborate on implementing the plan. I also came to understand that by accepting this, I was doing a disservice to my students with IEPs and 504 plans. Without a clear understanding of these plans, their goals, and my role in supporting their achievement within the classroom, I was not fully contributing to their development.

Upon this revelation, I approached the special education specialist and asked them to explain more clearly to me my role in the process, the target goals and behaviors, and the resources available. I am a visual learner, so I also asked the specialist to explain what I should see, what I should not see, and how I should approach specific situations. I learned a valuable lesson that day. In my case, had I not approached the special education teacher, I'm not sure how long the cyclical process of that teacher entering my classroom, calling the student to leave the classroom, and the student returning and needing to finish the assignments they'd had to leave behind to attend the session with the special education teacher would have continued. If I had not approached the special education teacher, I wouldn't have learned the importance of:

- Documenting each student's IEP goals and 504 services in a spreadsheet including the student's name and age, a timeline, strategies implemented, what worked/didn't work, who is involved, and action steps
- Using a variety of resources to educate myself and help students build executive function skills
- Partnering with each child's family to ensure they feel supported and understand the goals, services provided, and strategies implemented so that the plan extends beyond the school and classroom walls, to ensure consistent care

This last point is an important one, as often racially and ethnically diverse families are less able to advocate for their children and are left out of the process, do not understand the process, or, if they do advocate for their children, are treated as though they are at fault. Families want to know that they are not alone in navigating special education services for their children and must understand that they are a vital part of the team.

Understanding ADHD

The challenges diverse families face in advocating for their children become particularly evident when examining specific diagnoses that commonly lead to IEPs. One such diagnosis is attention-deficit/hyperactivity disorder (ADHD), which provides a critical lens through which to examine these disparities. To understand how race intersects with ADHD diagnosis and treatment, it's important to first explore the condition itself.

ADHD is a neurodevelopmental condition characterized by persistent patterns of inattention and/or hyperactivity and impulsivity that interfere with a child's ability to function in academic, social, or everyday settings (National Institute of Mental Health, n.d.). Genetics is recognized as the most common cause of susceptibility to ADHD, but other common risk factors include prenatal exposure to toxins and certain maternal metabolic conditions, prenatal hypoxia-ischemia, environmental factors, and some medical conditions. These factors may impact neuropsychological processes, leading to symptoms of this diagnosis (Batshaw et al., 2019, p. 356). ADHD is diagnosed through a clinical evaluation that integrates information from a comprehensive history, a physical and neurological examination, and an academic assessment (Batshaw et al., 2019, p. 358). To ensure a comprehensive evaluation, information must be obtained from multiple sources: family members and other caregivers, pediatricians, psychologists, teachers, specialists, and so on.

The symptoms are typically observed from a young age and persist into adulthood. However, research suggests that they are often perceived differently across racial and ethnic groups, which can lead to biases in diagnosis, treatment, and the support provided to students—especially Black and Brown children. Approximately one in three children that are diagnosed with ADHD receive the diagnosis in preschool (Hart et al., 2017). Approximately half of students who have been diagnosed with ADHD have IEPs or Section 504 plans (DuPaul et al., 2019). Research indicates that race can have a significant influence on decisions related to ADHD diagnoses (Cénat et al., 2021), with Black children more likely to be diagnosed with ADHD compared to their White and Latino peers (Zablotsky & Alford, 2020). A potential contributing factor here is that while children of all races typically exhibit similar symptoms, the behaviors of Black children are often perceived more negatively (Gilliam et al., 2016; Okonofua & Eberhardt, 2015). As I mentioned earlier, I witnessed this myself with my own daughter, who at the age of 3 was excluded from classroom activities for being "unable" to sit still, whereas when her White peer exhibited the same behavior, he was invited to sit in the teacher's lap or allowed to move freely around the room. With these considerations in mind, it is important to examine the reasons and processes for diagnosing young children with ADHD.

Some may argue that the behaviors exhibited by young children that lead to these diagnoses are actually developmentally appropriate for their age group. Others may argue that racial discrimination and bias play a role in overidentifying and diagnosing Black and Brown children with ADHD during the early years (Kang & Harvey, 2020). Careful consideration, with an understanding of brain research and child development as well as a critical evaluation of one's own assumptions and biases, is therefore crucial before recommending that young children be assessed for ADHD. Overidentification and misdiagnosis can have a negative impact on children's social-emotional development and learning (Kang & Harvey, 2020). Furthermore, when behaviors stem from a child's basic needs not being met, using strategies that are not appropriate, either developmentally or for addressing the root cause, can exacerbate inequities such as misidentification and misdiagnosis.

After a diagnosis is made, individualized goals should be set for the child, determined by the needs of that child and their family (Jimenez & Guevara, 2013). Because the core features of ADHD are difficulty sustaining mental effort, hyperactivity, and impulsivity, effective accommodations and interventions based on the goals set are imperative. Dietary modifications, exercise, meditation, yoga, mindfulness, and training in executive function skills each serve as intervention strategies that can accommodate the needs of a child who is diagnosed with ADHD (Batshaw et al., 2019, p. 371). Research highlights the importance of intentionally assessing and using a strengths-based approach to meet the needs of the whole child, shifting the focus away from the disability and toward "the abilities, talents, and skills of the child . . . and how to use those strengths to promote success" (Mindes & Jung, 2015, p. 127).

I learned the importance of dietary modifications as a teacher when one of my first-grade students was diagnosed with ADHD. At lunch each day, he drank a Coca-Cola. After informally assessing his behavior,

I noticed that it tended to change after lunch. It became harder for him to focus; he became easily distracted and off-task. One day, I approached this student's mother, with whom I had developed a reciprocal partnership through our weekly dialogues and check-ins. I asked her if she would be open to experimenting with removing the Coca-Cola from his lunch for a week. I suggested that she try reducing or eliminating other items containing large amounts of sugar from his diet during that time as well. We discussed the goal of the experiment and scheduled a follow-up meeting to review my observations. During that week, I noticed that my student had a much easier time maintaining focus in the afternoon. When I checked in with his mother, she confirmed that she had also eliminated sugary foods at home and had observed a noticeable difference in his behavior.

Accommodations for students with ADHD include shortening assignments without changing the difficulty level; providing written, visual, multistep directions; providing assistance writing assignments in a daily planner; and exercises to train executive function skills (Batshaw et al., 2019, p. 672). Other typical accommodations and modifications are redesigning the classroom environment in a way that considers spacing, colors, sounds, and smells; creating predictable schedules; and implementing movement breaks. With appropriate structures, routines, and equitable expectations that are consistently enforced, students can acquire the executive function and self-regulation skills that will help them avoid getting stuck in the preschool-to-prison pipeline and lead to positive learning outcomes.

ADDRESSING BEHAVIOR CHALLENGES WITH CHILD GUIDANCE/BEHAVIOR SUPPORT PLANS

Each early childhood setting will implement specific behavior management programs and intervention strategies, such as creating behavior support, student support, or child guidance plans, to identify and provide necessary supports for challenging behaviors in the classroom. In my experience with behavior support plans, the educator typically completes a checklist documenting the strategies they have tried with the student, and the behavior support team meets with the teacher to determine appropriate interventions. Ideally, however, the behavior support team will also assist the early educator with identifying relevant assessments, goals, and resources, model effective behavior management techniques, provide coaching for the teacher, and collaborate with them to determine the best methods to support both the student and the teacher.

In any approach adopted in a school setting, it is essential to consider multiple factors when assessing a child's behavior. However, it is crucial to begin by reflecting on whether the child's basic needs are being met. If they are not, determine how best to address those needs. Building a relationship with the child and their family can provide valuable insight into their home situation. Additionally, documenting the timing of the behavior, its frequency, and any potential triggers (such as interacting with specific peers or content areas) can help to better understand the root causes of the behavior.

The team should include a trusted staff member or adult who is assigned to the child. This could be a teacher, a school counselor or social worker, a front office administrator, a specialist, or another staff member. It should be someone with whom the child has or can build a strong relationship—someone they feel safe talking with, confiding in, and expressing their emotions to. This trust-based relationship should be nurtured throughout the school year. Remember, though, this trusted adult should not be the *only* person the child feels they can safely approach during difficult times. For instance, a first-grade boy named Miguel developed a trusting relationship with the school counselor. His parents were in the midst of a divorce, and during school hours he expressed his anger about the recent changes. The school counselor set out to develop a relationship with Miguel and his mother, and after a year of her consistently demonstrating that she would provide the support he needed, Miguel began to trust her. One day, when Miguel felt distracted in class, he used the strategies he had learned from the counselor: he reached into his backpack, took out his visual feelings chart, and approached his teacher. He then pointed to the visual of the school counselor, indicating his need to visit her office.

CONCLUSION

Early childhood educators must have a comprehensive understanding of the role of appropriate assessments and the processes involved in conducting and implementing the educational goals outlined in an IEP. It's also crucial for educators to distinguish between an IEP and a 504 plan. Equally important is recognizing the value of collaboration with the child's team—including specialists, administrators, instructional assistants, and the child's family—to effectively support the child's unique needs. This collaborative approach ensures that the child's academic, social, and emotional needs are met through coordinated efforts. Teachers must also employ specific strategies when working with children who have IEPs or 504 plans to ensure their needs are addressed appropriately. Appropriately addressing the diverse needs of young students begins by understanding the IEP and 504 process and by providing the necessary supports that promote development and learning.

CHAPTER 9

Leveraging Technology Tools

I want to ask you about using technology with preschool students. I don't like using it with my preschoolers because I know that this population of students are on their gadgets a lot when they get home from school. However, I have one child recently diagnosed with ADHD. I separated him a few weeks ago because he cannot control his body or hands. He has cut a child's hair. He also has spit on the other children at his table. So, part is behavior and part is the ADHD. He doesn't stay seated; he needs to walk around the room and cannot stay focused on the carpet. I am thinking that incorporating technology would help engage him in the lessons. I have come to the belief that maybe incorporating technology into my lessons is better than calling admin, which removes him from the class. Do I have another option?

—Question from a teacher

○ ○ ○

Digital technologies have the potential to transform education for all students, enabling children with a range of abilities to participate in activities and experiences in inclusive classroom settings. By integrating technology tools into the classroom, educators can create numerous opportunities to boost student engagement and motivation, fostering a more positive and productive learning environment. This chapter explores how developmentally appropriate technology resources can be used to equitably support curriculum, instruction, and assessment practices, guided by the principles of Universal Design for Learning.

TECHNOLOGY AND UDL

As NAEYC and the Fred Rogers Center for Early Learning and Children's Media (2012) observe in their position statement on technology and interactive media as tools in early childhood programs, all technology resources are not created equal; in particular, they warn that "noninteractive media can lead to passive viewing and overexposure to screen time for young children and are not substitutes for interactive and engaging uses of digital media or for interactions with adults and other children" (p. 2). Incorporating technology as a formal or informal form of assessment or intervention can often involve independent learning that focuses on "drill and practice" principles (Jack & Higgins, 2019)—picture four preschool-aged children, each placed strategically in front of their individual screens, provided with headphones, listening and responding to the content streaming from their computers. Thus, these tools are often seen as isolating and unengaging (Cordes & Miller, 2000) and a poor substitute for face-to-face interactions.

However, NAEYC and the Fred Rogers Center (2012) also acknowledge that "technology and interactive media are tools that can promote effective learning and development when they are used intentionally by early childhood educators, within the framework of developmentally appropriate practice . . . to support learning goals established for individual children" (p. 5). When integrated in a way that utilizes a developmentally appropriate, strengths-based approach, technology engages and empowers all learners by providing access to the curriculum (Keengwe & Onchwari, 2009). Indeed, when technology is used in this way, prioritizing assessments that illuminate student growth and learning; supporting acceleration of learning, not remediation; and shifting away from a model of independently answering and memorizing content to a collaborative approach that promotes active learning and higher order thinking, it can transform learning, giving young children varied opportunities to critically evaluate, discuss, explore and experiment with content (Darling-Hammond et al., 2020). It can also provide valuable real-time information to teachers about what instructional practices are working and what needs to be adjusted and reassessed.

Technology and Assessments

The International Society for Technology in Education (ISTE) Standards for Educators are a framework that guides teachers in integrating technology into the classroom. The standards emphasize the skills and qualities desired for students to engage and thrive in a digital world by challenging them to be agents of their own learning (Williams, 2019, p. 171). ISTE (2017) recommends that educators "[explore] proven and promising practices that leverage technology to improve student learning" (p. 4) and "facilitate learning with technology to support student achievement" (p. 5). Standard 7b states that educators should "use technology to design and implement a variety of formative and summative assessments that accommodate learner needs, provide timely feedback to students and inform instruction" (p. 5).

In the early childhood classroom, it is important that assessment practices be ongoing and seamlessly integrated into the daily routine and each lesson to measure development and learning. By incorporating technology tools into active learning, educators create continuous assessment opportunities that help measure the impact of these tools on each individual child's progress.

NAEYC (2020, p. 22) states that educators should aim to implement a comprehensive curriculum that enables each child to attain individualized goals across all learning domains and content areas, integrating the three principles of UDL. Technology offers vast opportunities to provide multiple means of engagement, representation, and action and expression for diverse learners. It can be used for pre-assessments, ongoing assessments, and post-assessments, for purposes such as teaching content, assessing learning, experimenting and creating, and engaging learners (Odhiambo, 2016, p. 48).

For pre-assessments, select technology tools that engage students across all three dimensions: behavioral (what they are doing), emotional (how they are feeling), and cognitive (what they are learning). These tools can also be used to continuously assess whether students are grasping the material, engaging with the content, making connections, and meeting learning objectives. The data gathered should inform decisions, provide appropriate supports, and guide next steps. For post-assessments, choose technology tools that allow all students to demonstrate their learning. Ensure there are diverse opportunities for students to engage in self-reflection, collaborate, and give and receive peer feedback.

Technology and Active Learning

Active learning invites students to fully participate in their learning by providing choice and opportunities to reflect, discuss, investigate, explore, experiment, and create (Center for Teaching Innovation at Cornell University, n.d.). Universal Design for Learning encourages active learning by intentionally integrating multiple means of engagement, representation, and action and expression, providing children with diverse opportunities to demonstrate knowledge, application, and understanding.

Integrating different technology tools within the early childhood classroom is one way of doing this, and it helps ensure that all students can access and engage in learning. Intentionally choosing technology tools and resources that promote active rather than passive learning supports the development of higher order thinking skills, which require multiple opportunities to understand, connect, and apply knowledge (Thomas & Thorne, 2009). It also increases the chances of maximizing positive emotions, which has a beneficial effect on development and learning—as discussed previously, research shows that affective states influence key aspects of learning, such as attention, memory, and motivation, and thus that emotional state impacts a person's readiness to learn (CISL, n.d.; Sousa, 2009). Early educators can choose developmentally appropriate technology tools and resources that promote active engagement, for example by engaging young children in creating stories, illustrating ideas, producing presentations, conducting research, creating podcasts, exploring questions, finding answers, and collaborating with others (Bullard, 2016).

If we refer to this chapter's opening vignette, while the teacher's statement and assessment included subjective language, they can be commended for assessing the child, reflecting on the child's needs, and recognizing that the strategies they were currently using to engage and connect with him were not working. Although the teacher's beliefs about the appropriateness of integrating technology during the early years were conflicting, they knew that they needed to address this child's needs. The next step in their reflective process would be to explore and choose developmentally appropriate technology tools that would promote engagement, representation, and action and expression. As Faith Rogow (2023) puts it, we must move from a model that is focused on the effects and impact of technology to one that is centered around teaching and learning and intentional use of technology.

CHOOSING TECHNOLOGY TOOLS

Technology integration can be defined as the use of technology resources, such as computers, mobile devices like smartphones and tablets, digital cameras, social media platforms and networks, software applications, the internet, and so on, in daily classroom practices to support learning (Gilbertson, 2007). In other words, it involves the incorporation of instructional and educational technology into the curricular, instructional, and assessment practices within the classroom. ISTE (2017) states that strategic technology integration can enhance educational outcomes, support development and learning, and transform teaching. Indeed, transforming and redefining how we teach can be viewed as the goal of technology integration (Gilbertson, 2007). By intentionally choosing technology tools that meet the developmental and individual needs of each young child, we can break down some of the barriers diverse young children often face during the early years of school.

However, as the previous section suggests, when planning this integration and selecting technology tools, it is important to consider the difference between tools that support active versus passive learning. In general, tools that support passive learning:

- disseminate information and ask students to simply answer questions or match words or pictures
- are isolating, relying on independent work
- utilize a drill and practice method
- are not developmentally appropriate—they may be too easy or too challenging, or not accessible or easy to navigate

In contrast, tools that support active learning:

- are interactive
- promote collaboration
- provide opportunities for students to make choices, experiment, and make mistakes
- reflect and integrate relevant learning domains and content areas

Integrating technology into the classroom in a transformative way requires incorporating it as more than a toy, but rather a tool that helps to promote critical thinking, reflection, and citizenship. The Universal Design for Learning framework encourages educators to utilize research on how young children learn best and to reflect upon their knowledge of how best to engage and motivate learners to inform and adapt environmental and curricular decisions in a way that ensures learning opportunities are accessible for all. The UDL principles provide a way to think systematically about curricular and instructional decisions such as technology integration to transform learning (Hartmann & Weisner, 2016).

From a UDL perspective, questions to ask while considering what technology tools to integrate into your classroom include:

- How can I engage my students by using technology (engagement)?
- How can I use technology to present information in ways that will reach all learners (representation)?
- How can I offer purposeful technology options for students to demonstrate what they know (action and expression)?

As you explore the use of technology tools in your classroom, I invite you to utilize the Emotions, Attention, Learning, Start over (EALS) checklist in Table 9-1. The checklist marries knowledge about child development and the UDL principles with Anita Archer and Charles Hughes's (2011) effective and efficient teaching strategies—I do, we do, and you do—and asks you to reflect on each tool you choose to integrate into the early childhood curriculum. The aim of these tools should be to capitalize on each child's positive emotions by activating prior knowledge and promoting the engagement of every learner.

Presenting content utilizing engaging technology resources (representation), providing the necessary time and varied opportunities for students to collaborate and develop an understanding of the content (engagement), and providing opportunities for students to demonstrate their learning using various technology resources (action and expression) encourages active and engaged learning.

TABLE 9-1. The EALS Checklist

Emotions (anticipatory set)	Did the selected technology tool provide opportunities for students to experience positive emotions from the beginning of the lesson? Was the anticipatory set presented in a relevant and engaging way?
Attention ("I do" and representation)	Was the content presented using a variety of technology tools and methods, considering the diverse learning styles of each student to enhance or transform their learning and development?
Attention ("we do" and engagement)	Did the technology tool offer opportunities for students to work together, provide different types of activities/choices, and give students the time and repetition needed to access the content?
Learning ("you do" and action and expression)	Did the tool incorporate a choice of options to allow the students to show their learning in different ways?
Start over (closure, restate and reflect)	Have I reflected on the learning that took place and created a new objective/goal based on student learning?

TECHNOLOGY TOOLS TO PROMOTE MULTIPLE MEANS OF ENGAGEMENT, REPRESENTATION, AND ACTION AND EXPRESSION

Here are a few examples of how you can use different technology tools in the classroom to support the UDL principles:

- Use GoNoodle, a free, research-based tool that gets kids moving with short interactive activities (multiple means of engagement).
- Use Sock Puppets, a free app designed to allow students to make puppet shows with voiceovers (multiple means of representation).
- Use Edpuzzle, a free app that uses videos to engage students in reflection, questions, and collaboration (multiple means of action and expression).

Tables 9-2 through 9-4 provide additional examples of technology resources that can be helpful for communicating with families, promoting classroom engagement (by facilitating interactive learning, encouraging participation, and supporting differentiated instruction to meet students' diverse needs), and conducting formative assessments. These lists are by no means exhaustive, and there are many other excellent tools available. I encourage you to explore and experiment to find what works best in your classroom setting.

TABLE 9-2. Technology Tools for Communicating with Families

TOOL	DESCRIPTION
Bloomz (www.bloomz.com)	A unified communication platform that aims to enhance the home-to-school connection by linking families with the classroom, school, and district
Seesaw (https://web.seesaw.me)	An interactive learning platform where teachers, families, and students can upload videos, documents, reminders, and other materials to promote communication and collaboration
Wixie (https://wixie.com)	A creativity platform for students that enables easy sharing of work with families

TABLE 9-3. Technology Tools for Teachers to Promote Engagement

TOOL	DESCRIPTION
ChatterPix Kids (available on the App Store and Google Play)	Allows animation with drawings, still photographs, etc. Young children can then record a message and watch the animation come alive.
Explee (https://explee.com)	An easy-to-use tool that allows teachers and students to create interactive and engaging animated videos and presentations
Powtoon (www.powtoon.com)	Allows children to create videos, animations, and presentations.
simpleshow (https://videomaker.simpleshow.com)	A video maker platform that makes creating engaging explainer videos for lessons simple
Sock Puppets app (available on the App Store)	Allows children to create stories using puppets and record voiceovers to make the puppets come alive.

TABLE 9-4. Technology Tools to Use for Formative Assessments

TOOL	DESCRIPTION
Blooket (www.blooket.com)	A gamified learning platform where teachers host games with various question sets and students answer on their own devices
Edpuzzle (https://edpuzzle.com)	An online editing tool that lets teachers create lessons based on videos, with voiceovers, questions and answers, and other features
Fix and Play (https://www.youtube.com/@fixandplay826)	A YouTube channel providing activity ideas, brain breaks, and "Would you rather?" games

THE ROLE OF TECHNOLOGY WITHIN THE EARLY CHILDHOOD ENVIRONMENT

Technology can have a positive impact on the learning environment and open up significant possibilities for supporting learners. However, it is important for early childhood educators to incorporate knowledge about child development and brain research to ensure they create environments that support technology integration in developmentally appropriate ways (Rosen & Jaruszewicz, 2009). The early childhood classroom environment should be a safe environment built around the belief that all members are valued and respected and are allowed and encouraged to explore, make mistakes, develop, and learn.

ISTE (2017) Standard 5 states that educators should design "authentic, learner-driven activities and environments that recognize and accommodate learner variability" (p. 5). More specifically, ISTE recommends that teachers:

5a. Use technology to create, adapt and personalize learning experiences that foster independent learning and accommodate learner differences and needs.

5b. Design authentic learning activities that align with content area standards and use digital tools and resources to maximize active, deep learning.

5c. Explore and apply instructional design principles to create innovative digital learning environments that engage and support learning.

When used intentionally, technology leads to a culture of social learning by empowering students of all abilities (Cicconi, 2014). Additionally, the use of assistive technology devices and services can help children with disabilities to actively engage and participate in learning and social interactions in the classroom (ECTAcenter.org, 2021). Common examples include support boards, adapted books, and voice output communication devices (Skau & Cascella, 2006). A well-designed learning environment recognizes the importance of embracing, including, and supporting all students' abilities. Intentionally integrating tools and resources that help with that into the everyday schedule and routines helps ensure that all students feel safe, included, and encouraged to take risks and participate.

The UDL principles of representation, engagement, and action and expression can be utilized to reflect upon and ensure that the chosen technology tools and resources are accessible and adaptable, providing equitable opportunities for each student to participate and contribute to the classroom environment. This supports young children's ability to access content through varied instructional strategies that provide opportunities to learn, develop, and connect (DEC & NAEYC, 2009). Such an environment recognizes the role young children play in serving as a producer of content and co-creators of their development and learning.

Successful integration of technology tools and resources is achieved when the use of technology meets the following four criteria (Gilbertson, 2007) to support and encourage relationship building, social and emotional development, and learning:

Part of the classroom routine (temporal environment)

Ensure that technology tools and resources chosen are part of the daily schedule and routine. For example, Reading Is Fundamental's interactive literacy calendars (available at www.rif.org/literacy-central/calendars) could be utilized during the sharing portion of the morning meeting or circle time, or you could use a resource such as Wheel of Names or Picker Wheel in lieu of equity sticks.

Accessible

Ensure equitable access to the technology tools and resources by choosing tools that can be differentiated and adapted to meet each child's goals and needs and promote participation. For example, you could use a visual classroom timer such as the ones available at www.online-stopwatch.com/classroom-timers/ so all students can see how much time is remaining for a particular activity, or integrate a tool like RoomRecess.com's interactive clock (www.roomrecess.com/Tools/InteractiveClock/play.html) for students who need practice with the math concept of telling time.

Supports the curriculum

To support and enhance the curriculum and ensure access is equitable, choose and incorporate various types of technology tools that are developmentally, individually, and culturally appropriate and adapted to students' interests and abilities.

Supports each child's goals

Ensure equitable supports are in place that are individualized for each child by conducting ongoing formative assessments, collaborating with colleagues, specialists, and family members, and using the resulting information to reflect upon and inform instructional and environmental decisions. For example, https://goformative.com is a free resource that allows educators to track student progress.

A high-quality, responsive learning environment embraces an inclusive teaching approach by cultivating a community of learners within a physically and emotionally safe environment. An inclusive classroom environment, characterized by a supportive school and classroom culture and climate and positive relationships, thus meets students' basic needs of safety and belonging and leads to deeper learning and reduced behavioral problems (Jones & Khan, 2017). Technology plays a supporting role in this type of environment by enabling ongoing collaborative experiences built on the knowledge that young children need appropriate time, space, and opportunities to interact, engage, explore, and experiment with content. This type of space is designed to elicit positive emotions where trust is established and students feel secure. "The setting must promote not only children's learning but also their pleasure in learning and the motivation to pursue it" (Epstein, 2014, p. 13).

Table 9-5 gives some examples of how technology tools, when combined with intentional decisions about the classroom environment, can enhance the curriculum and improve learning outcomes for all students, across various learning domains: social-emotional, cognitive, physical, and linguistic. Again, these are by no means exhaustive lists of the tools available in each domain; my intention here is simply to provide a few examples that can serve as a starting point. I encourage you to explore, experiment, and interact with different tools to find what best meets the needs of your students.

TABLE 9-5. Technology Integration Across Learning Domains

LEARNING DOMAIN	PHYSICAL ENVIRONMENT	INTEGRATING TECHNOLOGY	EXAMPLE TOOLS AND RESOURCES
Social and emotional development	Create inviting whole-group and small-group areas that include various-sized rugs and flexible seating options.	Provide multiple opportunities for students to set goals and accomplish them by working as a whole group, in small groups or pairs, and independently. Technology resources used to facilitate this work can be incorporated into the classroom routines.	• Book Creator app • Moody Me app
Cognitive development	Utilize centers within the PK–3 classroom environment: a math center, a science center, a library center, a writing center.	Utilize technology resources that provide varied experiences and will accommodate and support each child, enabling exploration and offering opportunities to ask questions, solve problems, and make decisions.	• Blooket (www.blooket.com) • BrainPOPJr. (https://jr.brainpop.com) • deck.toys (https://deck.toys) • Gimkit (www.gimkit.com) • Sutori (www.sutori.com/en/teachers) • ToonyTool (www.toonytool.com)
Physical development (gross and fine motor skills)	Include areas that provide opportunities to develop fine motor skills (pinching, cutting, writing, etc.) and areas that promote gross motor development (through activities such as dancing, walking, running, skipping, and hopping).	Provide multiple opportunities for engagement, representation, and action and expression.	• Fine motor: Toy Theater (https://toytheater.com) • Gross motor: Cosmic Kids Yoga (www.youtube.com/user/CosmicKidsYoga), GoNoodle (www.gonoodle.com)

LEARNING DOMAIN	PHYSICAL ENVIRONMENT	INTEGRATING TECHNOLOGY	EXAMPLE TOOLS AND RESOURCES
Language development (receptive and expressive)	Integrate quality, diverse children's literature within each area/center of the classroom, exploring diversity, identities, gender, race, class, and various types of families, experiences, cultures, and beliefs. Choose content that provides both a window (a view of others' lives, cultures, etc. that may be different from their own) and a mirror (a view that reflects students' own lives, cultures, etc.). Provide a dramatic play area to encourage imaginative play and learning.	Use your understanding of each child's interests and strengths to set goals that are individually appropriate and to engage students with the concepts in a way that resonates with them, incorporating various technology tools. In the dramatic play area, you might use a cash register to simulate a grocery store, allow students to create their own podcasts, or use laptops to simulate dining at a restaurant. Students can design their own menus and even develop QR codes to create an interactive experience. These activities not only encourage creativity but also provide opportunities for students to engage with technology in meaningful and context-rich ways.	• Dragon Anywhere speech-to-text app • Funbrain (www.funbrain.com/books) • Google Arts & Culture (https://artsandculture.google.com) • Newsela (https://newsela.com) • Oddizzi (www.oddizzi.com) • Puppet Pals 2 app

CONCLUSION

Integrating technology into the classroom helps address inequitable access by offering all students opportunities to explore a variety of tools and resources. These include digital cameras, video recorders, computers, laptops, and other technologies that support project-based learning, web-based activities, game-based learning, and research. Such integration ensures that every student has equitable access to engage in and demonstrate understanding through varied methods and resources that promote growth and development. Technologies such as apps, collaborative online tools, and social media platforms like TikTok can be used as instructional and assessment tools to promote varied opportunities for exploration and creation of products like podcasts, videos, or slideshows, increasing learners' engagement and motivation (Bullard, 2016; Gilbertson, 2007). In addition, assistive technologies can help level the playing field and ensure content, tasks, and activities are accessible to all students.

When selecting technology tools and resources, key questions to consider include:

- How do the methods support the learning goals?
- How can students learn about and select flexible methods?
- How are feedback and reflection on the methods incorporated into instruction?

Incorporating technology in the classroom in a way that embraces and integrates the principles of UDL can help foster optimal learning experiences. This approach allows learners to engage with tasks and assessments in ways that leverage their individual strengths, experiences, and goals (National Academies of Sciences, Engineering, and Medicine, 2018). To dismantle the educational inequities faced by diverse and marginalized students during the early years, educators must move beyond passive strategies that fail to engage learners or address their needs, interests, or strengths. Instead, they must capitalize on and embrace resources that encourage active engagement and learning. As Rogow (2023) notes, "What children are doing with media technologies is a much more salient variable than time spent on the technology. Effective education is not about counting screen minutes; it is about making screen minutes count" (Rogow, 2023).

Reflecting on this chapter's opening vignette, it's clear why the teacher was hesitant about using technology in the classroom. However, with the right developmentally appropriate tools, technology can enhance learning and support the growth of young students.

CHAPTER 10

Becoming a Reflective Educator

Bobby, a 3-year-old, attends a private preschool. This is Bobby's first year in school, as he was previously looked after at home and taught by his grandmother. His mother has received multiple calls with reports about Bobby's inability to self-regulate, expressing concern that he has been biting other students and throwing tantrums. Bobby's teachers have warned her that if his behavior does not improve, he will be expelled from the school.

Bobby's mother has tried to explain that he has recently been experiencing big changes in his life: they've just moved to a new house, he has a new baby sister, and this is his first experience in school. She asks that the school be patient and try to understand why he might be acting out. Despite her pleas, the phone calls with negative reports continue. And the more the calls continue, the more she notices that Bobby's attitude toward school has begun to change.

○ ○ ○

An antiracist early educator understands that being antiracist is an ongoing, challenging process requiring time, reflection, action, and repetition. To advocate for equitable policies, practices, and investments that ensure all children can thrive, it's vital to be informed about current issues related to early care and education (Bucher et al., 2023).

Early childhood education is arguably the most critical stage in a child's educational journey. While I may have some bias here as an early educator myself, research backs this up, showing that early academic failures can make it much harder for students to succeed in later grades (García & Weiss, 2015). Studies also show that children who face barriers in education may mentally "check out" as early as first grade (Fields et al., 2017). However, early childhood educators themselves often face significant challenges—low compensation, limited time, high demands, mandated requirements, negative school culture and climate—that make it harder to advocate for equitable opportunities for racially, ethnically, and otherwise marginalized students.

According to Bucher et al. (2023), to be effective advocates early educators must:

- understand both the strengths and needs of your community to secure support and resources centered around equity
- commit to studying and practicing antiracist, anti-bias, strengths-based educational approaches so that your advocacy efforts pursue racial and social justice
- be present, attentive, and reflective (p. 11)

Paulo Freire believed that empowerment is capable of transforming both relationships and the broader social and political landscape, and he envisioned a type of equality where all individuals are empowered (Veugelers, 2017). Early educators who are deeply committed to creating equitable learning and development opportunities for diverse students intentionally recognize and honor their intersectionalities, such as culture, race, ethnicity, religion, disability status, socioeconomic class, sexual orientation, and gender identity (essentially, the whole child). These educators actively work to dismantle practices and policies that prevent certain students from accessing vital opportunities for learning, growth, empowerment, and success (Lalor, 2022).

Given that 90 percent of brain development occurs before kindergarten (Brown & Jernigan, 2012), ensuring equitable access to high-quality early childhood education for diverse children is crucial for their future academic success. This is accomplished by breaking down the systemic barriers that stand in the way of our young diverse and marginalized students and their families; by continuously reflecting on our own biases, expectations, and school and classroom policies and practices; and by taking action and co-creating pedagogical approaches that are built on antiracist, anti-bias, strengths-based philosophies. Students enter early childhood schools and classrooms with their whole selves. We cannot eliminate their identities and experiences, and we should not seek to do so.

Young marginalized students are frequently punished for what they don't bring to the school and classroom environment, for what they don't know, and for the behaviors they exhibit in reaction to the injustices they experience. Like Bobby, the student in this chapter's opening vignette, many young students are punished for not knowing how to "do" school. Young students don't need more police, more security officers, authoritarian administrators, or scripted curriculum. They don't need repeated suspensions or visits to the principal's office at ages as young as 3 or 4 years old. What are these experiences signaling? That they don't belong, that they aren't worthy, that they can't, shouldn't, and don't fit in. As Morris (2022) says, "The emphasis on punishment has produced systems of learning that stifle creativity, undermine the development of critical thinking skills, and prime students for criminalization" (p. 117).

Early educators, school leaders, counselors, and related staff who understand and actively reflect on antiracism principles are better equipped to address their students' social-emotional development. These educators take intentional steps to build relationships, make meaningful connections, and utilize their knowledge of brain research and child development to support students' social and emotional growth. By doing so, they create an environment where all children, especially those from marginalized communities, can thrive emotionally and academically. Keeping the students' needs at the forefront of all school-wide decisions is key to making school a safe place where students, educators, and families work as a team and differing opinions and philosophies are expected and encouraged. The mental and physical well-being of students must be made a priority by considering and embracing all of their individual qualities and needs—physical, emotional, social, and intellectual—and their impact on learning (McLeod, 2024).

School systems can be transformed and can overcome and eradicate the institutional racism, injustices, and challenges faced by racially and ethnically diverse students. However, transforming trajectories requires collaborating with all key stakeholders. A school culture and climate that is positive and caring, where strong, trusting bonds between adults and children are not only possible but are deliberately created and expected as part of the school norm, helps to counter the barriers that prevent learning and development (Yu & Cantor, 2014).

Becoming an antiracist educator or leader is a continuous, ongoing process of reflection, evaluation, collaboration, and implementation of intentional strategic plans to meet each child's needs for academic learning. School leaders and educators can use the following checklist to reflect upon the process of advocacy:

- Collaborate with other administrators to provide and receive support related to antiracism work.
- Collaborate with community thought leaders.
- Collaborate with families, inviting, acknowledging, and including their voices in the planning and decision-making process.
- Provide all staff with encouragement and repeated opportunities for reflection.
- Listen carefully in discussions with staff, and keep notes documenting the date, time, topics of conversation, and next steps.
- Consider when to let go and delegate responsibilities.
- Utilize various forms of communication (X, Instagram, website, text messages, apps, etc.) to reach the school community. For example, create 5-minute weekly video messages (using tools such as Loom) and invite staff members and students to discuss topics relevant to the identified needs of students and their families.
- Utilize professional development opportunities to co-create action plans about dealing with trauma and building resiliency.

- Utilize free, local resources, and share those resources with families via various platforms.
- Utilize community organizations, and invite representatives of those organizations to speak to staff and families.

ACTION STEPS

Implementing the principles of UDL—providing multiple means of engagement, representation, and action and expression—is one way for teachers to promote learning and development, by intentionally providing supports that are tailored to children's individual needs. This approach ensures that each child can make academic progress and avoids the risk of some students falling behind. Through guided discovery, early educators can design experiences that help children make connections and build understanding of concepts and content via interactions with people and objects (Kostelnik et al., 2019).

Every child is unique, and each demonstrates knowledge and understanding in different ways. UDL provides a framework to enhance and optimize teaching and learning for all students by considering the "why," "what," and "how" of learning (Meyer et al., 2014). Educators must learn about each child's interests and strengths and use that information to guide instruction and to design a meaningful, engaging curriculum that sparks interest and motivation for learning and supports development.

Here are some key steps to remember when working with children:

Build a positive, welcoming, and inclusive community.

Administrators and educators should focus on creating a positive school and classroom culture and climate. It's important to involve all staff and stakeholders in co-facilitating this process. A strong sense of community encourages all students to support each other, helping ensure their basic needs for safety, security, and belonging are met.

Learn each child's triggers.

Educators need to understand what triggers each child. When you learn to recognize a child's triggers, you can hold regular check-ins. Pay attention to the signs, and communicate early and often. Be flexible and patient as you experiment with different strategies. You might need to step out of your comfort zone, and it might take days, weeks, or even months to discover what works best. Taking time to understand a child's triggers helps build a sense of physiological and psychological safety. Ask questions like:

- How was your night/morning/ride to school?
- Is there something you need help with?
- Did someone make you feel sad or angry?

Work as a team.

After reflecting on your assumptions, thoughts, instructional methods, and assessment practices and working to develop relationships with each child and learn their triggers, decide who else to involve in the process. This might include the school counselor, the child's family, previous teachers, administrators, and specialists. Working as a team, you can explore and share strategies to support the child's development of self-esteem. This, in turn, fosters resiliency and promotes self-actualization.

Partner with families.

This is crucial for creating collaborative relationships built on trust and respect between everyone involved in a child's development and learning. Consider the following questions to guide your partnerships with families:

- How are assessments and goals communicated and shared with families?
- Does everyone understand the identified plan to scaffold the child's learning and development?

Bailey et al. (2006) outline five key areas in the pathway to family empowerment:

- Families are able to articulate their children's abilities and needs.
- Families have a clear understanding of their rights and are encouraged to advocate for their children.
- Families acquire and apply strategies that facilitate their children's development.
- Families have access to support systems and actively utilize them.
- Families are connected to and have access to services and programs available in their communities.

TRAJECTORY + TEAMWORK + TIME = TRANSFORMATION

We must be patient with ourselves, the process, and the outcomes, but also understand the urgency of the need to reevaluate the ways racially, ethnically, and otherwise marginalized students and their families are viewed, listened to, acknowledged, and empowered within the school system during the early years and beyond. Students and their families do not need to learn to conform, to be "fixed" or to assimilate to the norms of the school; instead, they need to feel a sense of safety, belonging, and respect (Morris, 2022). Ultimately, we have no control over outside factors that our students and their families experience and bring into the school setting; however, we do have control over our own beliefs, assumptions, and practices. "All students have a mix of strengths and weaknesses, and we should celebrate that and not use those differences to label students" (Novak, 2016, p. 68). Positive social and emotional development and learning outcomes depend on the relationships formed, the trust developed, the alignment of goals for learning, the type of content to be learned, the use of developmentally appropriate practices, the characteristics and needs of learners, the inclusion of families, and the support available for learners and instructors (National Academies of Sciences, Engineering, and Medicine, 2018).

I can remember always getting in trouble in kindergarten and first grade for talking too much. I attended early childhood and elementary school in the South, and I used to get hit on the hand with a ruler for talking too much. Ironically, I was also diagnosed with a speech delay as a toddler and received speech and language services. My trajectory wasn't positive, as I was labeled as talkative and identified as incapable of achieving at the same level as my typically developing peers. However, my second-grade teacher collaborated with my mother and the speech therapist, and collectively, over time and with additional resources and strategies, I began to meet the set IEP goals. That second-grade year, my teacher, Mrs. Baker, cast me as the lead in the school play, *Sleeping Beauty*. It was because of that one teacher that my school trajectory was transformed.

An antiracist early educator empowers learners by co-creating affirming environments and individualizing the curriculum, instructional practices, and assessment approaches. When antiracist early educators implement the UDL principles, they are committing to intentionally implementing a strengths-based approach, incorporating developmentally, individually, culturally, linguistically, and ability-appropriate policies, practices, and strategies, that builds on and utilizes knowledge about child development and brain research. This creates the ideal conditions to transform developmental and learning outcomes.

The early school years are formative, as young children's experiences play a crucial role in shaping their academic identities and developing their self-esteem. The experiences children have during these years have a significant impact on their perceptions of school and learning and the way they engage in learning throughout their later school years. The stories and voices of teachers, children, and families shared in the vignettes throughout this book not only highlight the fact that not all children have equitable access to high-quality early childhood experiences, but also demonstrate the intentionality of many early educators who, with courage, acknowledge that they do not have all the answers and recognize the need for support in accommodating the diverse developmental and learning needs within the schools and classrooms they serve.

When early educators give up on, label, or set low expectations for young children, they risk causing these children to lose their enthusiasm for school and learning. When this happens during the early years, it becomes much harder to reignite that passion and joy for learning later—especially during middle and high school, when many students struggle with in-school trauma. It's important not to play the blame game when solutions don't work. As Kendi (2019) observes, "Self-critique allows change" (p. 214). In other words, educators should continuously reflect on their practices, assess what is and isn't working, and make the necessary adjustments. Learning and development take time—they don't happen after just one lesson, no matter how great or well prepared it may be.

Above all, our young students want to

- trust and feel safe in their school and classroom community, and be comfortable taking risks and making mistakes;
- develop self-confidence and self-esteem through repeated opportunities to develop and progress; and
- have their voices heard and acquire techniques and strategies that will assist them in expressing their feelings, emotions, needs, and wants.

"Brains in pain cannot learn," as Lori Desautels (2016) has noted. Remember that when a student experiences trauma, doesn't feel as though they are welcome or belong in their school context, or is having a hard time accessing learning, time and repetition are needed to rewire the brain from old, negative thought patterns and habits of mind (conscious and unconscious). An effective and intentional educator understands that positive relationships and interactions stem from the environment, the classroom design and setup, and a collaborative and welcoming classroom community and culture. As has been observed previously, emotion drives attention, and attention drives learning. An antiracist educator prioritizes social and emotional development by applying insights from brain research and child development, while using UDL principles to counter barriers that hinder learning. This approach transforms practices and policies to ensure that all students have equitable opportunities for joyful, developmentally rich early learning experiences.

One year, while working as a professor at New York University in the early childhood education program, I taught a multicultural education course. I decided to ask my master's-level students whether they had ever invited their prekindergarten to third-grade students, who were from the lower and mid-west side of New York City, to voice their opinions and provide their feedback about their school and classroom experiences. My graduate students were stunned: "What? Why would we ask little ones for advice and feedback?" one replied. So, I challenged them to a task of asking the young students they served what makes a good teacher. As you read a few of the responses they received, ask yourself: What's your motivation for working in the early childhood education field? What questions would you ask the students you work with about their schooling experiences?

Here are some of the young students' responses, in their own words (misspellings and all):

> *Dear..., *
>
> *I think you should first get to know all of there names first. Then after that you should ask them what they like. Also that you should only yell when you need to and make shour that they always get along.*

> *Dear..., *
>
> *What makes a teacher good is when they don't put too much pressure on the kid because then he gets freaked out and scared. And maybe a place for the children to chill out.*

> *Dear..., *
>
> *Don't give homework on fridays.no yelling, and the most important of all is be a very good teacher.*

Dear ... ,

Here are some tips to be a very good and nice teach. Always be patience and ask the children if they need help with anything.

Dear ... ,

Don't be so hard on the students
Give stickers
Have independent reading
No homework on Friday
Get all information students will need
Always remember students names

Dear ... ,

What makes a good teacher:
A person who makes learning fun
Help explain misunderstood work

CONCLUSION

What better way to conclude this book than by reflecting on the wisdom of young students themselves? Children offer a wealth of insights, as they are acutely aware of their surroundings and the treatment they receive. They understand instinctively whether their environments meet their basic needs and how they are valued within them. As early educators, we hold the most crucial responsibility; the experiences young children have during these formative years lay the foundation for their future success. It should be our goal that every child who enters an early childhood classroom receives an equitable opportunity to continuously experience the excitement, pleasure, and joy of learning.

Antiracism must be active, not passive. Universal design has to be intentionally implemented—not just intended. Success for all must be more than passion. It has to be power by empowerment!

—Andratesha Fritzgerald in
*Antiracism and Universal Design for Learning:
Building Expressways to Success*

APPENDIX

Additional Resources for Educators

The following is a non-exhaustive list of organizations committed to meeting the needs of diverse students and their families. Early childhood school leaders and educators can use this list as a starting point for continuing dialogue, exploration, and reflective practice.

ORGANIZATION	WEBSITE
Arts on the Horizon	https://www.artsonthehorizon.org
Association of Children's Museums (ACM)	https://childrensmuseums.org
Breathe for Change	https://www.breatheforchange.com
Center for Educational Improvement (CEI)	https://www.edimprovement.org
Center for Transformative Teaching and Learning	https://www.thecttl.org
Center on Inclusive Technology and Education Systems (CITES)	https://cites.cast.org
Center on the Developing Child at Harvard University	https://developingchild.harvard.edu
Classroom Assessment Scoring System (CLASS)	https://teachstone.com/class/
Colours of Us	https://coloursofus.com
Conscious Discipline	https://consciousdiscipline.com

ORGANIZATION	WEBSITE
Council for Exceptional Children (CEC)	https://exceptionalchildren.org
Crisis and Trauma Resource Institute	https://ca.ctrinstitute.com/resources/printable-handouts/
Childhood Education International (CEI)	https://ceinternational1892.org
Early Childhood Art Educators (ECAE)	https://www.arteducators.org/community/articles/67-early-childhood-art-educators-ecae
Early Childhood Music Education	https://nafme.org/resource/early-childhood-music-education
EdSource	https://edsource.org
Housman Institute	https://www.housmaninstitute.com
Inclusive Schools Network	https://inclusiveschools.org
International Society for Technology in Education (ISTE)	https://iste.org
Kennedy Center	https://www.kennedy-center.org
Learning for Justice	https://www.learningforjustice.org
National Association for Gifted Children (NAGC)	https://nagc.org
National Association for Family, School, and Community Engagement (NAFCSE)	https://nafsce.org
National Association for Multicultural Education (NAME)	https://www.nameorg.org
National Association for Music Education (NAfME)	https://nafme.org
National Council for the Social Studies (NCSS)	https://www.socialstudies.org
National Council of Teachers of Mathematics (NCTM)	https://www.nctm.org
National Science Teaching Association (NSTA)	https://www.nsta.org
Responsive Classroom	https://www.responsiveclassroom.org

ORGANIZATION	WEBSITE
Seek Common Ground (SCG)	https://seekcommonground.org/family-guides
Society of Health and Physical Educators (SHAPE America)	https://www.shapeamerica.org
U.S. Department of Education	https://www.ed.gov

REFERENCES

Adamu, M., & Hogan, L. (2015). *Point of entry: The preschool-to-prison pipeline*. Center for American Progress. https://cdn.americanprogress.org/wp-content/uploads/2015/10/08000111/PointOfEntry-reportUPDATE.pdf

Alanís, I., Arreguin, M., & Salinas-Gonzalez, I. (2021). *The essentials: Supporting dual language learners in diverse environments in preschool and kindergarten*. NAEYC.

Alanís, I., & Sturdivant, T. (2023). *Focus on developmentally appropriate practice: Equitable and joyful learning in preschool*. NAEYC.

Alleman, J., & Brophy, J. (1999). *Current trends and practices in social studies assessment for the early grades*. National Council for the Social Studies. www.socialstudies.org/sites/default/files/publications/yl/

Allen, K., & Cowdery, G. (2015). *The exceptional child: Inclusion in early childhood education*. Cengage.

Bacher-Hicks, A., Billings, S. B., & Deming, D. J. (2019). *The school-to-prison pipeline: Long-run impacts of school suspensions on adult crime*. NBER Working Paper 26257. www.nber.org/system/files/working_papers/w26257/w26257.pdf

Bailey, B. (2014). *Conscious discipline: Building resilient classrooms*. Loving Guidance.

Bailey, D. B., Jr., Bruder, M. B., Hebbeler, K., Carta, J., Defosset, M., Greenwood, C., Kahn, L., Mallik, S., Markowitz, J., Spiker, D., Walker, D., & Barton, L. (2006). Recommended outcomes for families of young children with disabilities. *Journal of Early Intervention, 28*(4), 227–251. https://doi.org/10.1177/105381510602800401

Ball, R. A. H. (2006). Supporting and involving families in meaningful ways. *Young Children, 61*(1), 10–11. http://www.jstor.org/stable/42729859

Barron, L., & Kinney, P. (2021). *We belong: 50 strategies to create community and revolutionize classroom management*. ASCD.

Bateman D., & Cline, J. (2016). *A teacher's guide to special education*. ASCD.

Batshaw, M., Roizen, N., & Pellegrino, L. (2019). *Children with disabilities* (8th ed). Paul H. Brookes Publishing Co.

Belsky, G. (2024). *The 3 areas of executive function*. Understood. www.understood.org/en/articles/types-of-executive-function-skills

Bhandari, C., & Douglas, S. N. (2024). Embedding mindfulness into early childhood classroom routines: A practical strategy for teachers. *Childhood Education Innovations, 100*(4), 20–29. https://ceinternational1892.org/wp-content/uploads/2024/07/EmbeddingMindfulness.pdf

Birth To 5 Matters. (n.d.). *Self-regulation*. https://birthto5matters.org.uk/self-regulation/

Bohn, J. (2017). *4 ways to create a positive school culture*. ASCD. https://ascd.org/blogs/four-ways-to-create-a-positive-school-culture

Brown, T. T., & Jernigan, T. L. (2012). Brain development during the preschool years. *Neuropsychology Review, 22*(4), 313–333. https://doi.org/10.1007/s11065-012-9214-1

Buchanan, T., & LeMoyne, T. (2020). Helicopter parenting and the moderating impact of gender and single-parent family structure on self-efficacy and well-being. *The Family Journal, 28*(3), 262–272. https://doi.org/10.1177/1066480720925829

Buchanan-Rivera, E. (2022). *Identity affirming classrooms: Spaces that center humanity*. Routledge.

Bucher, E., Clark, K., & Larkin, K. A. (2023). The power in our collective voices: Building your skills as an early childhood advocate. *Young Children, 78*(2). www.naeyc.org/resources/pubs/yc/summer2023/power-collective-voices

Bullard, J. (2016). *Creating environments for learning: Birth to age 8* (3rd ed.). Pearson.

Cantor, P., Darling-Hammond, L., Irby, M., & Pittman, K. (2021). *How can we design learning settings so that all students thrive?* SoLD Alliance. www.soldalliance.org/post/how-can-we-design-learning-settings-so-that-all-students-thrive

Canty-Barnes, E. (2016). *Racial inequality starts in preschool*. The New Republic. https://newrepublic.com/article/135071/racial-inequality-starts-preschool

Carey, L., & Reid, A. (2024). *Supporting student executive functions: Insights and strategies for educators*. CAST Professional Publishing.

CARF. (1998). *What is institutional racism?* Institute of Race Relations. https://irr.org.uk/article/what-is-institutional-racism/

CASEL. (n.d.). *A supportive classroom environment*. https://schoolguide.casel.org/focus-area-3/classroom/a-supportive-classroom-environment/

CAST. (2018). *UDL and the learning brain*. www.cast.org/products-services/resources/2018/udl-learning-brain-neuroscience

Causton, J., & MacLeod, K. (2020). *From behaving to belonging: The inclusive art of supporting students who challenge us.* ASCD.

CCTASSI (Center for Child Trauma Assessment, Services and Interventions). (n.d.). *What is child trauma?* https://cctasi.northwestern.edu/child-trauma/

CDC (Centers for Disease Control and Prevention). (2019). *Promoting parent engagement: Improving student health and academic achievement.* www.cdc.gov/healthyyouth/protective/factsheets/parentengagement_administrators.htm

CDC (Centers for Disease Control and Prevention). (2024). *About adverse childhood experiences.* www.cdc.gov/aces/about/

Cénat, J. M., Blais-Rochette, C., Morse, C., Vandette, M.-P., Noorishad, P.-G., Kogan, C., Ndengeyingoma, A., & Labelle, P. R. (2021). Prevalence and risk factors associated with attention-deficit/hyperactivity disorder among US Black individuals: A systematic review and meta-analysis. *JAMA Psychiatry, 78*(1), 21–28. https://doi.org/10.1001/jamapsychiatry.2020.2788

Center for Teaching Innovation at Cornell University. (n.d.) *Active learning.* Retrieved December 20, 2024, from https://teaching.cornell.edu/teaching-resources/active-collaborative-learning/active-learning

Children's Defense Fund. (2023). *State of America's children.* www.childrensdefense.org/tools-and-resources/the-state-of-americas-children/soac-education/

Cicconi, M. (2014). Vygotsky meets technology: A reinvention of collaboration in the early childhood mathematics classroom. *Early Childhood Education Journal, 42,* 57–65. http://dx.doi.org/10.1007/s10643-013-0582-9

CISL (Center on Inclusive Software for Learning at CAST). (n.d.). *Affect & student learning.* https://cisl.cast.org/research/affect-student-learning

Clark, R., Anderson, N. B., Clark, V. R., & Williams, D. R. (1999). Racism as a stressor for African Americans: A biopsychosocial model. *American Psychologist, 54*(10), 805–816. https://doi.org/10.1037/0003-066X.54.10.805

Conkbayir, M. (2017). *Early childhood and neuroscience: Theory, research and implications for practice.* Bloomsbury Academic.

Cordes, C., & Miller, E. (2000). *Fool's gold: A critical look at computers in childhood.* Alliance for Childhood. https://eric.ed.gov/?id=ED445803

Darling-Hammond, L., Schachner, A., & Edgerton, A. K. (2020). *Restarting and reinventing school: Learning in the time of COVID and beyond.* Learning Policy Institute. https://restart-reinvent.learningpolicyinstitute.org/sites/default/files/product-files/Restart_Reinvent_Schools_COVID_REPORT.pdf

Davis, B. (2021). *Holding students back—An inequitable and ineffective response to unfinished learning.* EdTrust. https://edtrust.org/resource/holding-students-back-an-inequitable-and-ineffective-response-to-unfinished-learning

DEC (Division for Early Childhood of the Council for Exceptional Children). (2007). *Promoting positive outcomes for children with disabilities: Recommendations for curriculum, assessment, and program evaluation.* www.decdocs.org/position-statement-promoting-positi

DEC (Division for Early Childhood of the Council for Exceptional Children). (2020). *The EI/ECSE Standards (2020).* www.dec-sped.org/ei-ecse-standards

DEC & NAEYC (Division for Early Childhood of the Council for Exceptional Children & National Association for the Education of Young Children). (2009). *Early childhood inclusion.* www.naeyc.org/sites/default/files/globally-shared/downloads/PDFs/resources/position-statements/ps_inclusion_dec_naeyc_ec.pdf

Desautels, L. (2016). *Brains in pain cannot learn!* Edutopia. www.edutopia.org/blog/brains-in-pain-cannot-learn-lori-desautels

Dobbins, D., McCready, M., & Rackas, L. (2016). *Unequal access: Barriers to early childhood education for boys of color.* https://themoriahgroup.com/wp-content/uploads/2023/02/fb2077_ccec9ec43bdc4c399d811091517b3bde.pdf

Drinks, T. (2019). *When do kids start sitting still?* Understood. www.understood.org/en/articles/when-do-kids-start-sitting-still

Duchesneau, N. (2020). *Social, emotional, and academic development through an equity lens.* EdTrust. https://edtrust.org/wp-content/uploads/2014/09/Social-Emotional-and-Academic-Development-Through-an-Equity-Lens-August-6-2020.pdf

DuPaul, G. J., Chronis-Tuscano, A., Danielson, M. L., & Visser, S. N. (2019). Predictors of receipt of school services in a national sample of youth with ADHD. *Journal of Attention Disorders, 23*(11), 1303–1319. https://doi.org/10.1177/1087054718816169

ECTAcenter.org (2021). *Improving systems, practices, and outcomes.* https://ectacenter.org/decrp/topic-environment.asp

Epstein, A. (2014). *The intentional teacher: Choosing the best strategies for young children's learning.* NAEYC.

Erdman, S., Colker, L., & Winter, E. (2020). *Trauma and young children: Teaching strategies to support and empower.* NAEYC.

Estrada, J. D., & Popp, S. (2024). 4 pillars of school mental health. *Educational Leadership, 81*(5). https://ascd.org/el/articles/4-pillars-of-school-mental-health

Fields, M., Meritt, P., & Fields, D. (2017). *Constructive guidance and discipline: Birth to age 8*. Pearson.

Fisher, D., & Frey, N. (2023). Five peer tutoring strategies for the classroom. *Educational Leadership, 81*(2). https://ascd.org/el/articles/five-peer-tutoring-strategies-for-the-classroom

Freire, P. (1973). *Education for critical consciousness* (1st American ed.). Seabury Press.

Fritzgerald, A. (2020). *Antiracism and Universal Design for Learning*. CAST Professional Publishing.

Gabbard, C. (1998). Windows of opportunity for early brain and motor development. *Journal of Physical Education, Recreation & Dance, 69*(8), 54–55. http://dx.doi.org/10.1080/07303084.1998.10605614

Gartrell, D. (2023). *Education for a civil society: Teaching young children to gain five democratic life skills* (2nd ed.). NAEYC.

Gatlin, B. T., & Wilson, C. L. (2016). Overcoming obstacles: African American students with disabilities achieving academic success. *The Journal of Negro Education, 85*(2), 129–142. https://doi.org/10.7709/jnegroeducation.85.2.0129

García, E., & Weiss, E. (2015). *Early education gaps by social class and race start U.S. children out on unequal footing*. Economic Policy Institute. www.epi.org/publication/early-education-gaps-by-social-class-and-race-start-u-s-children-out-on-unequal-footing-a-summary-of-the-major-findings-in-inequalities-at-the-starting-gate/

Garwood, J. D., & Carrero, K. M. (2023). Lifting the voices of Black students labeled with emotional disturbance: Calling all special education researchers. *Behavioral Disorders, 48*(2), 121–133. https://doi.org/10.1177/01987429221130729

Gerzel-Short, L., Kiru, E. W., Hsiao, Y.-J., Hovey, K. A., Wei, Y., & Miller, R. D. (2019). Engaging culturally and linguistically diverse families of children with disabilities. *Intervention in School and Clinic, 55*(2). https://doi.org/10.1177/1053451219837637

Gilbertson, N. (2007). *What is successful technology integration?* Edutopia. www.edutopia.org/technology-integration-guide-description

Gillespie, C. (2019). *Young learners, missed opportunities: Ensuring that Black and Latino children have access to high-quality state-funded preschool*. EdTrust. https://edtrust.org/wp-content/uploads/2014/09/Young-Learners-Missed-Opportunities.pdf

Gilliam, W. S., Maupin, A. N., Reyes, C. R., Accavitti, M., & Shic, F. (2016). Do early educators' implicit biases regarding sex and race relate to behavior expectations and recommendations of preschool expulsions and suspensions? *Yale University Child Study Center, 9*(28), 1–16. www.jsums.edu/scholars/files/2017/03/Preschool-Implicit-Bias-Policy-Brief_final_9_26_276766_5379.pdf

Goff, P. A., Jackson, M. C., Di Leone, B. A. L., Culotta, C. M., & DiTomasso, N. A. (2014). The essence of innocence: Consequences of dehumanizing Black children. *Journal of Personality and Social Psychology, 106*(4), 526–545. https://doi.org/10.1037/a0035663

Goldberg, M. (2012). *Arts integration: Teaching subject matter through the arts in multicultural settings* (4th ed.). Pearson.

Gruenert, S., & Whitaker, T. (2023). *School culture versus school climate*. ASCD. https://ascd.org/blogs/school-culture-versus-school-climate

Guy-Evans, O. (2023). *Primary and secondary emotions: Recognizing the difference*. Simply Psychology. www.simplypsychology.org/primary-and-secondary-emotions.html

Hammond, Z. (2014). *Culturally responsive teaching and the brain: Promoting authentic engagement and rigor among culturally and linguistically diverse students*. Corwin.

Hannaford, C. (2005). *Smart moves: Why learning is not all in your head* (2nd ed.). Great Ocean Publishers.

Hart, K., Ros, R., Gonzalez, V., & Graziano, P. (2017). Parent perceptions of medication treatment for preschool children with ADHD. *Child Psychiatry and Human Development, 49*, 155–162. https://doi.org/10.1007/s10578-017-0737-9

Hartmann, E., & Weisner, P. (2016). Technology implementation and curriculum engagement for children and youth who are deafblind. *American Annals of the Deaf, 161*(4), 462–473. https://doi.org/10.1353/aad.2016.0038

Hoerr, T. (2023). Developing your school "culture budget." ASCD. https://ascd.org/blogs/developing-your-school-culture-budget

Iruka, I. U. (2022). Delivering on the promise of early childhood education for black children: An equity strategy. *New Directions for Child and Adolescent Development*, 27–45. https://doi.org/10.1002/cad.20483

Institute of Education Sciences. (2023). *Common trauma symptoms in students and helpful strategies for educators*. https://ies.ed.gov/ncee/edlabs/regions/appalachia/events/materials/04-8-20-Handout3_common-trauma-symptoms-and-helpful-strategies-for-educators.pdf

IOM & NRC (Institute of Medicine & National Research Council). (2015). *Transforming the workforce for children birth through age 8: A unifying foundation*. The National Academies Press.

ISTE (International Society for Technology in Education). (2017). *ISTE standards for educators: A guide for teachers and other professionals.* https://iste.org/standards/educators

Jack, C., & Higgins, S. (2019). What is educational technology and how is it being used to support teaching and learning in the early years? *International Journal of Early Years Education, 27*(3), 222–237. https://doi.org/10.1080/09669760.2018.1504754

James, C., & Iruka, I. (2018). *Delivering on the promise of effective early childhood education.* National Black Child Development Institute. https://buildinitiative.org/wp-content/uploads/2021/06/Delivering-on-the-Promise-of-Effective-Early-Childhood-Education.pdf

Jimenez, M. E., & Guevara, J. P. (2013). A 7-year-old boy experiencing difficulty at school. *Canadian Medical Association Journal, 185*(15), 1333–1335. https://doi.org/10.1503/cmaj.130042

Jones, S. M., & Khan, J. (2017). *The evidence base for how we learn: Supporting student's social, emotional, and academic development.* The Aspen Institute National Commission on Social, Emotional, and Academic Development. www.aspeninstitute.org/wp-content/uploads/2017/09/SEAD-Research-Brief-9.12_updated-web.pdf

Kaiser, B., & Rasminsky, J. S. (2021). *Addressing challenging behavior in young children.* NAEYC.

Kang, S., & Harvey, E. (2020). Racial differences between Black parents' and White teachers' perceptions of attention-deficit/hyperactivity disorder behavior. *Journal of Abnormal Child Psychology, 48,* 661–672. https://doi.org/10.1007/s10802-019-00600-y

Kaufman, T. (2020). *Building positive relationships with students: What brain science says.* Understood. www.understood.org/en/articles/brain-science-says-4-reasons-to-build-positive-relationships-with-students

Keengwe, J., & Onchwari, G. (2009). Technology and early childhood education: A technology integration professional development model for practice teachers. *Early Childhood Education Journal, 37*(3), 209–218. http://dx.doi.org/10.1007/s10643-009-0341-0

Kendi, I. X. (2019). *How to be an antiracist.* Random House.

Kostelnik, M., Soderman, A., Whiren, A., & Rupiper, M. (2019). *Developmentally appropriate curriculum: Best practices in early childhood education* (6th ed.). Pearson.

Lalor, A. (2022). *5 elements of a relevant curriculum.* ASCD. www.ascd.org/el/articles/5-elements-of-a-relevant-curriculum

Lewis, K., Kuhfield, M., Ruzek, E., & McEachin, A. (2021). *Learning during COVID-19: Reading and math achievement in the 2020-21 school year.* NWEA Center for School and Student Progress. www.nwea.org/research/publication/learning-during-covid-19-reading-and-math-achievement-in-the-2020-2021-school-year/

Luby, J. L., Rogers, C., & McLaughlin, K. A. (2021). Environmental conditions to promote healthy childhood brain/behavioral development: Informing early preventive interventions for delivery in routine care. *Biological Psychiatry Global Open Science, 2*(3), 233–241. https://doi.org/10.1016/j.bpsgos.2021.10.003

Mahoney, J. L., Durlak, J. A., & Weissberg, R. P. (2018). *An update on social and emotional learning outcome research.* Kappan. https://kappanonline.org/social-emotional-learning-outcome-research-mahoney-durlak-weissberg/

McAfee, O., & Leong, D. (2015). *Assessing and guiding young children's development and learning* (6th ed.). Prentice Hall.

McInerney, M., & McKlindon, A. (2014). *Unlocking the door to learning: Trauma-informed classrooms and transformational schools.* Education Law Center. www.elc-pa.org/wp-content/uploads/2015/06/Trauma-Informed-in-Schools-Classrooms-FINAL-December2014-2.pdf

McLeod, S. (2024). *Maslow's hierarchy of needs.* Simply Psychology. www.simplypsychology.org/maslow.html

Meek, S., Iruka, I. U., Allen, R., Yazzie, D., Fernandez, V., Catherine, E., McIntosh, K., Gordon, L., Gilliam, W., Hemmeter, M. L., Blevins, D., & Powell, T. (2020). *Fourteen priorities to dismantle systemic racism in early care and education.* The Children's Equity Project. https://cep.asu.edu/sites/default/files/2021-12/14-priorities-equity-121621.pdf

Meloy, B., Gardner, M., & Darling-Hammond, L. (2019). *Untangling the evidence on preschool effectiveness: Insights for policymakers.* Learning Policy Institute. https://learningpolicyinstitute.org/product/untangling-evidence-preschool-effectiveness-report

Meyer, A., Rose, D., & Gordon, D. (2014). *Universal Design for Learning: Theory & practice.* CAST Professional Publishing.

Meyer, A., Rose, D., & Gordon, D. (2024). *Universal Design for Learning: Principles, Framework, and Practice.* CAST Professional Publishing.

Milner, H. R., IV. (2019). Race to improve teacher education: Building awareness for instructional practice. *American Educator, 43*(3), 13–17. www.aft.org/sites/default/files/media/2019/ae-fall2019.pdf

Milner, H. R., IV, Cunningham, H. B., Delale-O'Connor, L., & Kestenberg, E. G. (2019). *"These kids are out of control": Why we must reimagine "classroom management" for equity*. Corwin.

Mindes, G., & Jung, L. (2015). *Assessing young children* (5th ed.). Pearson.

Moll, L. C. (1992). Bilingual classroom studies and community analysis: Some recent trends. *Educational Researcher, 21*(2), 20–24. https://doi.org/10.3102/0013189X021002020

Morgan, H. (2020). Misunderstood and mistreated: Students of color in special education. *Voices of Reform, 3*(2), 71–81. https://doi.org/10.32623/3.10005

Morris, M. (2022). *Cultivating joyful learning spaces for Black girls: Insights into interrupting school pushout*. ASCD.

NAEP (U.S. Department of Education Institute of Education Sciences, National Center for Education Statistics, National Assessment of Educational Progress). (2022a). *NAEP report card: Mathematics*. https://www.nationsreportcard.gov/mathematics/?grade=4

NAEP (U.S. Department of Education Institute of Education Sciences, National Center for Education Statistics, National Assessment of Educational Progress). (2022b). *NAEP report card: Reading*. https://www.nationsreportcard.gov/reading/?grade=4

NAEP (U.S. Department of Education Institute of Education Sciences, National Center for Education Statistics, National Assessment of Educational Progress). (2025a). *NAEP report card: Mathematics*. https://www.nationsreportcard.gov/reports/mathematics/2024/g4_8/performance-by-student-group/?grade=4

NAEP (U.S. Department of Education Institute of Education Sciences, National Center for Education Statistics, National Assessment of Educational Progress). (2025b). *NAEP report card: Reading*. https://www.nationsreportcard.gov/reports/reading/2024/g4_8/performance-by-student-group/?grade=4

NAEYC (National Association for the Education of Young Children). (1993). *A conceptual framework for early childhood professional development*. www.naeyc.org/sites/default/files/globally-shared/downloads/PDFs/resources/position-statements/PSCONF98.PDF

NAEYC (National Association for the Education of Young Children). (2009). *Developmentally appropriate practice in early childhood programs serving birth through age 8*. www.naeyc.org/sites/default/files/globally-shared/downloads/PDFs/resources/position-statements/PSDAP.pdf

NAEYC (National Association for the Education of Young Children). (2019a). *Advancing equity in early childhood education.* www.naeyc.org/sites/default/files/globally-shared/downloads/PDFs/resources/position-statements/advancingequitypositionstatement.pdf

NAEYC (National Association for the Education of Young Children). (2019b). *Professional standards and competencies for early childhood educators.* www.naeyc.org/sites/default/files/globally-shared/downloads/PDFs/resources/position-statements/standards_and_competencies_ps.pdf

NAEYC (National Association for the Education of Young Children). (2020). *Developmentally appropriate practice.* www.naeyc.org/sites/default/files/globally-shared/downloads/PDFs/resources/position-statements/dap-statement_0.pdf

NAEYC (National Association for the Education of Young Children). (2022). *Developmentally appropriate practice in early childhood programs serving children from birth through age 8* (4th ed.). NAEYC.

NAEYC (National Association for the Education of Young Children) & Fred Rogers Center for Early Learning and Children's Media at Saint Vincent College. (2012). *Technology and interactive media as tools in early childhood programs serving children from birth through age 8.* www.naeyc.org/sites/default/files/globally-shared/downloads/PDFs/resources/position-statements/ps_technology.pdf

National Academies of Sciences, Engineering, and Medicine. (2018). *How people learn II: Learners, contexts, and cultures.* The National Academies Press.

National Center on Safe Supportive Learning Environments. (n.d.). *Physical environment.* Retrieved December 20, 2024, from https://safesupportivelearning.ed.gov/topic-research/environment/physical-environment

National Institute of Mental Health. (n.d.). *Attention-deficit/hyperactivity disorder: What you need to know.* www.nimh.nih.gov/health/publications/attention-deficit-hyperactivity-disorder-what-you-need-to-know

National School Climate Council. (2009). *National school climate standards.* https://schoolclimate.org/wp-content/uploads/2021/05/school-climate-standards.pdf

NCES (National Center for Education Statistics). (2022). *Table 1. Public high school 4-year adjusted cohort graduation rate (ACGR), by race/ethnicity and selected demographic characteristics for the United States, the 50 states, the District of Columbia, and Puerto Rico: School year 2019–20.* https://nces.ed.gov/ccd/tables/ACGR_RE_and_characteristics_2019-20.asp

NCES (National Center for Education Statistics). (2024a). *Racial/ethnic enrollment in public schools*. Condition of Education. U.S. Department of Education, Institute of Education Sciences. Retrieved December 20, 2024, from https://nces.ed.gov/programs/coe/indicator/cge

NCES (National Center for Education Statistics). (2024b). *Students with disabilities*. Condition of Education. U.S. Department of Education, Institute of Education Sciences. Retrieved December 20, 2024, from https://nces.ed.gov/programs/coe/indicator/cgg

NCLD (National Center for Learning Disabilities). (2020). *Significant disproportionality in special education: Current trends and actions for impact*. https://ncld.org/wp-content/uploads/2023/07/2020-NCLD-Disproportionality_Trends-and-Actions-for-Impact_FINAL-1.pdf

Novak, K. (2016). *UDL now! A teacher's guide to applying Universal Design for Learning in today's classrooms* (2nd ed.). CAST Professional Publishing.

Novak, K., & Rodriguez, K. (2023). *How UDL creates an equitable environment for students*. Edutopia. www.edutopia.org/article/universal-design-learning-promotes-equity/

Novak, K., & Woodlock, M. (2021). *UDL playbook for school and district leaders*. CAST Professional Publishing.

Odhiambo, E., Nelson, L., & Chrisman, K. (2015). *Social studies and young children*. Pearson.

Okonofua, J. A., & Eberhardt, J. L. (2015). Two strikes: Race and the disciplining of young students. *Psychological Science, 26*(5), 617–624. https://doi.org/10.1177/0956797615570365

Owens, J., & McLanahan, S. S. (2020). Unpacking the drivers of racial disparities in school suspension and expulsion. *Social Forces, 98*(4), 1548–1577. https://doi.org/10.1093/sf/soz095

Pino-James, N. (2014). *Golden rules for engaging students in learning activities*. Edutopia. www.edutopia.org/blog/golden-rules-for-engaging-students-nicolas-pino-james

Posey, A. (2018). *Engage the brain: How to design learning that taps into the power of emotion*. ASCD.

Posey, A. (n.d.-a). *How to break down barriers to learning with UDL*. Understood. www.understood.org/en/articles/how-to-break-down-barriers-to-learning-with-udl

Posey, A. (n.d.-b). *Lesson planning for universal design for learning*. Understood. www.understood.org/en/articles/lesson-planning-with-universal-design-for-learning-udl

Rakesh, D., McLaughlin, K. A., Sheridan, M., Humphreys, K. L., & Rosen, M. L. (2024). Environmental contributions to cognitive development: The role of cognitive stimulation. *Developmental Review, 73*, 101135. https://doi.org/10.1016/j.dr.2024.101135

Rebora, A. (2022). *Beyond lip service on school well-being*. ACSD. https://ascd.org/el/articles/beyond-lip-service-on-school-well-being

Reynolds, J., & Kendi, I. X. (2020). *Stamped: Racism, antiracism, and you*. Little, Brown Books for Young Readers.

Rodriguez-Knutsen, A. (2023). *Types of racism: Internal, interpersonal, institutional, and structural*. YWCA. www.ywcaworks.org/blogs/ywca/types-racism

Rogow, F. (2023). Framing: How we think about our work. *Young Children, 78*(4). www.naeyc.org/resources/pubs/yc/winter2023/framing-our-work

Rose, D. H., & Meyer, A. (2002). *Teaching every student in the digital age: Universal Design for Learning*. ASCD.

Rosen, D. B., & Jaruszewicz, C. (2009). Developmentally appropriate technology use and early childhood teacher education. *Journal of Early Childhood Teacher Education, 30*(2), 162–171. https://doi.org/10.1080/10901020902886511

Roundtable on Community Change. (2017). *Glossary for understanding the dismantling structural racism/promoting racial equity analysis*. www.aspeninstitute.org/wp-content/uploads/files/content/docs/rcc/RCC-Structural-Racism-Glossary.pdf

Schiller, P. (1999). *Start smart: Building brain power in the early years*. Gryphon House.

Schlund, J. (2021). *What does "social emotional learning" really mean?* https://medium.com/social-emotional-learning/in-school-systems-around-the-world-theres-growing-appreciation-of-the-importance-of-social-and-fc797d8aa84

Seefeldt, C., Castle, S., & Falconer, R. (2013). *Social studies for the preschool/primary child* (9th ed.). Pearson.

Skau, L., & Cascella, P. W. (2006). Using assistive technology to foster speech and language skills at home and in preschool. *Teaching Exceptional Children, 38*(6), 12–17. https://doi.org/10.1177/004005990603800602

Sousa, D. (2022). *How the brain learns* (6th ed.). Corwin.

Sousa, D. (2009). *How the brain influences behavior: Management strategies for every classroom*. Corwin.

Stafford-Brizard, B. (2024). *The power of educator EQ*. ASCD. https://ascd.org/el/articles/the-power-of-educator-eq

Statman-Weil, K. (2015). *Creating trauma-sensitive classrooms*. NAEYC. www.naeyc.org/system/files/YC0515_Trauma-Sensitive_Classrooms_Statman-Weil.pdf

Sue, D. W. (2010). *Microaggressions in everyday life: Race, gender, and sexual orientation*. Wiley.

Teachstone. (n.d.) *The complete guide to CLASS*. https://teachstone.com/the-complete-guide-to-class/

Thibodeau, T. (2021). *The science and research behind the UDL framework*. Novak Education. www.novakeducation.com/blog/the-science-and-research-behind-the-udl-framework

Thomas, A., & Thorne, G. (2009). *How to increase higher order thinking*. Center for Development and Learning. Retrieved December 20, 2024, from www.readingrockets.org/topics/comprehension/articles/how-increase-higher-order-thinking

Toldson, I. A. (2020). Transdisciplinary convergence to accelerate strategies to mitigate institutional racism in criminal justice, education, and health systems. *The Journal of Negro Education, 89*(1), 1–7. https://doi.org/10.7709/jnegroeducation.89.1.0001

Tull, M. (2020). *Secondary emotions and post-traumatic stress disorder*. Verywell Mind. www.verywellmind.com/secondary-emotions-2797387

Understood. (n.d.) *What is a 504 plan?* understood.org/en/articles/what-is-a-504-plan

UnidosUS. (2022). *Latino student success: Advancing U.S. educational progress for all*. https://unidosus.org/wp-content/uploads/2022/07/UnidosUS_Latino-Education_2022.pdf

USDOE (U.S. Department of Education). (n.d.-a). *Frequently asked questions: Section 504 free appropriate public education (FAPE)*. www.ed.gov/laws-and-policy/civil-rights-laws/disability-discrimination/frequently-asked-questions-section-504-fape

USDOE (U.S. Department of Education). (n.d.-b). *Individuals With Disabilities Education Act (IDEA)*. www.ed.gov/laws-and-policy/individuals-disabilities/idea

USDOE (U.S. Department of Education). (2017). *Sec. 303.344 Content of an IFSP*. https://sites.ed.gov/idea/regs/c/d/303.344

USDOE (U.S. Department of Education). (2018). *Sec. 300.8 Child with a disability*. https://sites.ed.gov/idea/regs/b/a/300.8

USDOE (U.S. Department of Education). (2021). *Discipline practices in preschool*. Office for Civil Rights. https://ocrdata.ed.gov/assets/downloads/crdc-DOE-Discipline-Practices-in-Preschool-part1.pdf

USDOE (U.S. Department of Education). (2024). *Profile of students with disabilities in U.S. public schools during the 2020-21 school year.* Office for Civil Rights. www.ed.gov/media/document/crdc-student-disabilities-snapshotpdf

USDHHS & USDOE (U.S. Department of Health and Human Services & U.S. Department of Education). (2014). *Policy statement on expulsion and suspension policies in early childhood settings.* www.ed.gov/sites/ed/files/2020/07/policy-statement-ece-expulsions-suspensions.pdf

Veugelers, W. (2017). The moral in Paulo Freire's educational work: What moral education can learn from Paulo Freire. *Journal of Moral Education, 46*(4), 412-421. https://doi.org/10.1080/03057240.2017.1363599

Watson, A. (2022). *The most important 5 minutes in class: The primacy/recency effect.* Learning & the Brain. www.learningandthebrain.com/blog/the-most-important-5-minutes-in-class-the-primacy-recency-effect/

Watson, G. (2021). *3 ways to make a sense of belonging real and valuable.* Education Week. www.edweek.org/leadership/opinion-stop-telling-students-you-belong/2021/11

Williams, J. (2019). *Teach boldly: Using edtech for social good.* ISTE.

Wynter-Hoyte, K., & Smith, M. (2020). "Hey, Black child. Do you know who you are?" Using African diaspora literacy to humanize blackness in early childhood education. *Journal of Literacy Research. 52*(4) 406-431. https://doi.org/10.1177/1086296X20967393

Xie, H. (2013). Strengths-based approach for mental health recovery. *Iranian Journal of Psychiatry and Behavioral Sciences, 7*(2), 5-10. https://pmc.ncbi.nlm.nih.gov/articles/PMC3939995/

York, S. (2016). *Roots and wings: Affirming culture and preventing bias in early childhood.* Redleaf Press.

Yu, E., & Cantor, P. (2014). *Poverty, stress, schools: Implications for research, practice and assessment.* Turnaround for Children. https://turnaroundusa.org/wp-content/uploads/2016/05/Turnaround-for-Children-Poverty-Stress-Schools.pdf

Zablotsky, B., & Alford, J. M. (2020). *Racial and ethnic differences in the prevalence of attention-deficit/hyperactivity disorder and learning disabilities among U.S. children aged 3-17 years.* NCHS Data Brief 358. www.cdc.gov/nchs/data/databriefs/db358-h.pdf

Zeng, S., Corr, C. P., O'Grady, C., & Guan, Y. (2019). Adverse childhood experiences and preschool suspension expulsion: A population study. *Child Abuse and Neglect, 97,* 104149. https://doi.org/10.1016/j.chiabu.2019.104149

INDEX

A

abandonment, 21
abuse, childhood, 17
academic performance
    and class environment, 48
    early-life foundation for, 37–38, 170
    effect of trauma on, 39
    and family-school partnerships, 68
    motivation and belonging, 59
    national proficiency scores, 4–5
    unwanted behavior amidst, 43
    See also success, academic
academic self-esteem
    cultural bias vs., 11–12
    and discipline gap, 14
    early formation of, 176
    effect of punitive actions on, 6, 12, 15
    expectations and, 139
    in temporal environment, 81
    UDL-informed building of, 100, 102
action and expression
    case study of implementing, 36
    in family-school partnerships, 72
    in lesson plans, 104
    multiple means of, 87, 135
    6 E's approach, 100–104
    and technology, 155, 158–161
    UDL principle of, 33, 35
active learning, 81, 85–91, 156–157
ADHD (attention-deficit/hyperactivity disorder), 147–150
Advancing Equity in Early Childhood Education, 33
adverse childhood experiences (ACEs), 17–18
affective networks, 83–84
Ages and Stages Questionnaires (ASQ), 132
aggressiveness, 22
Alleman, Janet, 130
American Indian students. *See* racially and ethnically diverse students
anchor charts, 54, 55
anger, 22
Antiracism and Universal Design for Learning (Fritzgerald), 10, 180
antiracist education
    active teacher reflection in, 171
    in America, 29
    assessment practices in, 122
    creating equal opportunities via, 33, 35
    in early school years, 8, 31–32
    empowerment by, 176
    and family-school partnerships, 71
    fostering belonging in, 63
    and hierarchy of needs, 41
    intentionality for, 30–31, 175–180
    vs. one-size-fits-all curricula, 23
    as ongoing for teachers, 29, 30
    resources for, 181–183
    and response to misbehavior, 20–21, 169–170
    as strengths-based, 130
    and student variability, 43
    and UDL, 97
    welcoming classrooms for, 56
anxiety, 21
arrest, 4
arts, the, 90–91
assessments
    antiracist, 31
    barriers to appropriate, 127–129
    and child development, 132–133
    clarity about, 112–113
    cyclical, 130
    deficit approach to, 128–129

assessments (*continued*)
    defined, 122
    equality in, 9
    evaluation of, 134–136
    family input into, 73
    5 E's for, 133–136
    formative and summative, 122, 124, 126–127
    inclusive, 63
    in lesson plans, 104
    observation and, 116–117, 125, 126
    ongoing assessments, 131, 135–136
    purpose of, 122–126
    for self-regulation, 121
    state standards, 127–128
    strengths-based, 125–126, 130–131
    technology in, 155–156, 161
    three steps for, 124
    UDL-informed, 97
attendance, 5
attention
    in EALS checklist, 159
    emotions and learning, 15, 19, 42
    factors affecting, 82
attitudes toward learning
    mentally dropping out, 5
    and misbehavior, 22
    psychological safety and, 55–56

B

Bailey, Dr. Becky, 18
barriers to learning
    and assessment, 127–129
    in early education, 7
    eliminating, 31, 33–34, 37–38, 120
    exclusionary disciplines as, 5
    and family-school partnerships, 70, 74
    list of, 5
    meeting of basic needs and, 42
    one-size-fits-all curricula as, 24
    race/ethnic inequalities as, 5, 30
behavior
    and child guidance, 89–91
    and emotions, 32–33
    expectations for, 29, 88
    factors contributing to, 57

behavior, unwanted
    as call for help, 18
    and cultural proficiency, 10–11
    and "difficult" label, 15
    and eagerness to participate, 27
    and emotional upset, 3
    and life knowledge, 171
    and meeting of basic needs, 40–41
    and placement in special ed., 16
    reasons for, 21–22, 78–79
    support plans for, 150–151
    teacher files on, 13
    trauma and, 18, 19–21, 39
    and unequal treatment, 15
belonging
    and engaged learning, 60, 61–62, 177
    in Maslow's hierarchy of needs, 40, 42
    motivation and, 59
    ongoing cultivation of, 63
    in outdoor spaces, 55
    and use of wall space, 53–54
bias
    acknowledging personal, 31, 122
    active dismantling of, 37, 69, 171
    and ADHD diagnosis, 148–149
    and age perception, 28
    and assessments, 128, 129
    cultural. *See* cultural bias
    and disciplinary policies, 12–13
    effects of, 9
    in family-school partnerships, 69, 70
    institutionalized racism, 9
    and placement in special ed., 16
    in school policies, 4, 42
Black/Brown students. *See* racially and ethnically diverse students
Bloom's Taxonomy, 105
boredom, 43
brain, the
    and ADHD, 148
    choice and, 53
    and class routines, 81
    executive function, 83
    learning and networks of, 41

and stress responses, 39–40
and UDL principles, 83–84
brain development
    and ADHD diagnosis, 149
    classroom layout and, 48, 51
    early in life, 8, 50
    and equitable education, 170–171, 177
    and student assessment, 123, 132–133
    technology and, 165
Brophy, Jere, 130

C

calm spaces, 47, 57, 81
Cantor, Pamela, 24
childhood trauma, 17–18
Children's Defense Fund, 5
Classroom Assessment Scoring System (CLASS), 102
classroom environments
    the arts in, 90–91
    equality in, 9
    expectations for, 88
    family role in, 75
    and implicit curriculum, 49
    as safe/welcoming, 47–48
    See also physical classroom environment
climate, school. See school culture
clocks, interactive, 163
collaboration
    and active learning, 87
    and class layout, 56
    in family-school partnerships, 67
    on IEP team, 141
    and peer relationships, 60
    to roll out UDL, 114
confidence, student, 5, 53, 139
COVID-19 pandemic
    academic proficiency following, 4–5
    effects on racially and ethnically diverse students, 6
    trauma of, 18–19, 22
cradle-to-prison pipeline, 5
creativity
    and class layout, 47, 50, 51
    curricula lacking, 34
    role of the arts, 90–91
culpability, 28
cultural bias
    in family-school partnerships, 69
    and punishment of racially and ethnically diverse students, 10
    and special education, 16
    student sensitivity to, 49–50
    and systemic racism, 9, 10–12
cultural proficiency
    advocacy checklist for, 172–173
    and antiracist teaching, 31–32
    in assessments, 122
    and class materials, 61, 73
    and family variability, 69
    and implicit curriculum, 49
    and student variability, 37
    and UDL, 97
culture, school. See school culture
curriculum
    antiracist, 31–32
    cultural proficiency and, 61
    equality in, 9
    example of modifying, 35–37
    implicit and explicit, 49
    lesson plans, 103
    one-size-fits-all, 22–25, 125
    pacing/scripted, 34
    partnering with families on, 71–72
    relevant, 106–107
    for student variability, 23, 35
    and technology, 162–163
    temporal environment and, 78, 82
    trauma-informed, 40
    UDL-informed, 96, 97

D

dance, 91
David Goes to School (Shannon), 54
decision-making, 85
defense mechanisms, 15
Desautels, Lori, 177
developmentally appropriate practices
    and academic success, 14, 33–34
    of assessment, 122, 123, 132–133
    and class environment, 51

developmentally appropriate practices (*continued*)
    and curriculum goals, 23
    family input into, 72
    in inclusive classrooms, 63
    lack of, 34, 77
    and response to misbehavior, 20–21
    and social/emotional skills, 8, 85
    technology in, 154, 161
    in temporal environment, 80, 82–84, 91–92
    from warm demanders, 112
diet, 149–150
disabilities, students with
    ADHD, 147–150
    assessments for, 128
    IEPs for, 142, 143
    legal protection for, 143
    qualification as, 144–145
    race/ethnic statistics on, 5
    special education for, 15–16, 140
    unequal treatment of, 4
discipline gap, 13–14
distractions, reducing, 50, 56
diversity
    celebration of, 8, 25
    and strengths-based approach, 24–25
    student variability, 23
    and unequal treatment, 4
Division for Early Childhood of the Council for Exceptional Children (DEC), 97
divorce, 17, 151
documentation boards, 135
domestic violence, 17
dropping out, mentally, 6–7

E

EALS (Emotions, Attention, Learning, Start over) checklist, 159
early childhood education
    age-based class environments, 50–51
    antiracist, 30
    assessments in, 122–123, 131
    creating welcome in, 38
    defined, 7
    disadvantages in, 4–5
    essential role of, 7–9, 25, 56, 170, 176
    family input into, 72
    and human development, 8–9, 37
    and IEP development, 142–143
    inequality in, 6–7, 30
    one-size-fits-all, 23–24, 78
    scheduling in, 82
    strengths-based approach to, 24
    technology in, 161–166
    trauma-informed, 18, 40
    variability acknowledged in, 43, 119
Early Interventionist/Early Childhood Special Educator (EI/ECSE) Standards, 140
Edpuzzle, 160
Education Trust, 14, 25
educators
    in 504 process, 145–147
    antiracist education for, 30, 31–32
    both/and approach of, 8
    in class layout, 52
    collaborative team of, 114
    cultural proficiency of, 10–11, 122
    essential role of, 56–57
    and IEP development, 142–143, 152
    instructional practices of, 96–97
    mindfulness modeling by, 58, 60
    reflection by, 62–63, 104, 169–170
    resources for, 181–183
    and school culture/climate, 66
    teamwork between, 174
    trauma-informed, 18–21
    as warm demanders, 112
emotions
    and active learning, 87
    behaviors associated with, 21–22, 32, 78
    development and emotional skills, 8
    in EALS checklist, 159
    and learning, 15, 19, 42
    negative responses, 3
    primary and secondary, 19, 32–33, 40
    welcoming environments and, 56–60, 62–63
    See also social-emotional learning

empowerment, student, 99, 100, 102, 176
encouragement, 97, 100, 101
engagement
    assessments and, 134
    and the brain, 83–84
    case study of implementing, 36
    and class layout, 50, 51
    with early education, 8
    equitable, 116
    in family-school partnerships, 72
    in lesson plans, 104
    motivation and belonging, 59, 60
    multiple means of, 73, 87
    and psychological safety, 56
    6 E's approach to, 98–99
    technology and increased, 155, 158–161
    UDL principle of, 34
    and use of wall space, 53–54
    and variety of materials, 108
equity
    in early education, 8, 12, 170
    educator commitment to, 170, 176
    in engagement opportunities, 116
    intersectional factors, 69
    patient creation of, 175–179
    student observation of, 14
    and technology use, 166
ethnic groups
    ADHD diagnosis for, 148–149
    expulsion rates for, 5–6, 12
    and family-school partnerships, 69
    stereotypes about, 10–11
    unequal treatment of, 4–7, 9, 170
exclusionary discipline
    as barrier to learning, 5
    effect on racially and ethnically diverse students, 6–7, 13–15
    vs. participatory impulse, 29, 31
    reasons for, 10
    and systemic racism, 9
    unequal application of, 4, 12, 13–15, 16
executive function
    and ADHD, 149, 150
    and class layout, 52
    for goal-directed tasks, 105
    and routines, 111
    and technology use, 158
    and temporal environment, 80, 83
    and UDL guidelines, 98
    for young children, 78
expectations
    assessment and, 134
    and child development, 28, 132
    clarity about, 104
    differing family, 69
    for family-school partnerships, 71
    lowered, 15, 30, 177
    school/home mismatches in, 15, 25, 26
    and self-esteem, 139
    setting clear, 81, 88
    shaping behavioral, 89
    state standards, 127
    and student variability, 23, 24
    in temporal environment, 82
    wall-space demonstrations of, 54
explicit curriculum, 49
exploration, 8, 99, 100, 101
expulsion
    as ACE/trauma, 17–18
    as barrier to learning, 5
    effects on students, 13–15
    racial/ethnic statistics on, 5–6, 12
    from unwanted behavior, 169

F

family-school partnerships
    for assessments, 135
    barriers to, 69–74
    for behavioral support, 151
    curriculum input in, 71–72
    family discord and students, 38–39
    fostering, 73–74
    for IEPs, 140, 141–142
    relationship-building in, 67–68
    and school culture, 66, 74–75, 174–175
    technology in, 160–161
    trust in, 68
    and use of wall space, 53–54
fatigue, 39, 57
favoritism, 9
fear, 22

feedback
    from families, 70–73
    on IEPs, 146
    from students, 117–118, 178–179
Fields, Marjorie, 78
fight, flight, and freeze response, 39, 59
5 E's for assessment, 133–136
504 plans, 143–147
flexibility
    for action/expression, 135
    in assessment practices, 124
    with children's triggers, 174
    in class routines, 110–112
    flexible seating, 54–55, 61
    in instructional practice, 109–110
    of materials/resources, 107–109
    mental, 83
    technology and increased, 155
food, 57
formative assessments, 122, 124, 126–127, 155, 161
Fred Rogers Center for Early Learning and Children's Media, 154
Freire, Paulo, 30, 170
Fritzgerald, Andratesha, 10, 180

G

gaps
    addressing learning, 6, 26
    discipline gap, 13–14
    opportunity gaps, 25–26
gardens, 55
goals, curricula
    assessments and, 131
    clarity about, 104–107, 112
    developmentally appropriate, 23
    displayed on classroom walls, 53–54
    evaluation of, 99, 101, 102
    materials aligned with, 107–108
    for special education, 141, 142
    technology-supported, 163
    in UDL principles, 34
Goff, Phillip, 28
Goldberg, Merryl, 90
GoNoodle, 160

grade retention
    as ACE/trauma, 17–18
    as racially disproportionate, 12–13, 14–15
    and timely graduation, 5

H

Hammond, Zaretta, 6, 59
Hannaford, Carla, 56
help, calls for, 18
Hoerr, Thomas, 67
home life
    and behavioral considerations, 20
    diet at home, 149–150
    trauma in, 17
    See also family-school partnerships
How to Be an Antiracist (Kendi), 29

I

IEP (Individualized Education Program). *See* Individualized Education Program (IEP)
implicit curriculum, 49
incarceration, 4
inclusivity
    and belonging, 63
    in class materials, 61
    family input into, 68, 71, 73
    in physical classroom, 49, 51, 56
    via UDL principles, 34
Individualized Education Program (IEP)
    and ADHD, 147–150
    assessments in, 128
    behavioral challenges, 150–151
    development of, 142–143, 152
    family input into, 140
    and 504 plans, 143–147
    as legal contract, 141
    team collaboration in, 141–142
Individualized Family Service Plan (IFSP), 140
Individuals with Disabilities Education Act (IDEA), 5, 15, 140
inequality
    active deconstruction of, 30–31, 33
    compounding effects of, 10–11

effect on racially and ethnically diverse students, 6–7, 8
as experienced by young children, 10
of one-size-fits-all curricula, 24
and opportunity gaps, 25–26
perpetuation of, 29, 30
in punitive actions, 12, 13–14
in school policies, 4, 9
student observation of, 14, 32
systemic, 4–7
innocence, privilege of, 28
institutionalized racism
and cultural bias, 10–11
exclusionary discipline and, 12–13
intentional dismantling of, 25, 32
and low academic self-esteem, 11
manifestations of, 9–10
and one-size-fits-all curricula, 22–25
and placement in special ed., 15–16
and resource distribution, 13–15
society of, 30
and trauma, 17–22
instructional practices
assessment-informed, 128
clarity about, 112
of early childhood educators, 96–97
equality in, 175–176
family input into, 72
flexibility in, 109–110
pacing in. See temporal environment
UDL-informed, 97
intentionality
and ADHD, 149
of antiracist educators, 31
for assessments, 136–137
in family-school partnerships, 70
for inclusive classrooms, 62–63
in physical classroom, 50
interactive learning, 86
isolation
and disciplinary policies, 13–15
and misbehavior, 21
and technology, 154

J
Jones, Stephanie, 58
joy of learning
fostering, 8, 66, 179
in inclusive classrooms, 63
loss of, 7, 177
participation and, 29
and technology use, 164

K
Kaiser, Barbara, 39
Kendi, Ibram, 29
Khan, Jennifer, 58
knowledge
and active learning, 86
and assessment, 127–128
and exclusionary disciplines, 13–14
within families, 68
means for gaining, 26
for one-size-fits-all curricula, 24
and social/emotional skills, 8
of students, 179

L
language
cultural bias about, 10–11
development and technology, 166
multilingual options for families, 74
talkativeness, 11
Latinx students. See racially and ethnically diverse students
learning
active, 81, 85–91, 156–157
addressing gaps in, 4–5, 26
and the brain, 51, 53
and class layout, 51, 56
community of, 58–60
in EALS checklist, 159
and emotions, 15, 19, 42
and hierarchy of needs, 40–42, 56–57
loss of joy/excitement about, 7
movement and, 81
punitive actions and, 12
and relationship, 40
resistance to, 21
and school culture/climate, 66

learning (*continued*)
    student attitudes toward, 5, 22, 55–56
    and the temporal environment, 82
    trauma and impaired, 17–18, 177
    UDL and equality in, 96
    welcoming environments, 38
    See also safe learning spaces
lesson plans, 103–104, 112, 131
LGBTQIA+ students, 4
libraries, 47, 51, 52
life experience
    and antiracist education, 31, 171
    impact on learning, 35
    and student assessment, 133–134
    and student variability, 23–25
    in UDL implementation, 99, 100, 101
loneliness, 21
love, human need for, 40, 42

M

marginalized groups
    ADHD diagnosis in, 148–149
    advocacy checklist for, 172–173
    and assessment bias, 128
    equity challenges for, 170
    families as, 70
    school policy and inequality of, 4, 28
    in special education, 16
mascots, 91
Maslow, Abraham, 40
Maslow's hierarchy of needs
    families and, 69–70
    learning and, 56–57
    and physical class environment, 48
    and the temporal environment, 91
    trauma and, 39
materials, class, 61, 107–109
math assessments, 4
Meloy, Beth, 8
memory, working, 83, 111
mental flexibility, 83
mentally dropping out, 5, 7, 18, 31
Meyer, Anne, 34
microaggressions, 70
Milner, H. Richard, 17
mindfulness, 60
motor skills, 132, 165
movement, 28, 34, 81, 88, 150
music, 91

N

Nation's Report Card, 4
Native American students. *See* racially and ethnically diverse students
needs, hierarchy of, 39, 48
neglect, 17
noninteractive media, 154
Northwest Evaluation Association (NWEA), 6

O

Office for Civil Rights, 6, 12
ongoing assessments, 131, 135–136, 155
opportunities
    for all families, 70
    equal academic, 33–34
    gaps in, 25–26, 29, 71
    providing multiple learner, 113
    technology and, 153–154, 156, 167
outdoor areas, 51, 55

P

pacing of instruction, 87–88
    See also temporal environment
participation, 29, 56
passive learning, 86, 154
patience, 39, 40, 175–179
pets, class, 55
physical classroom environment
    creating welcome in, 47
    effects of, 62
    and engaged learning, 61
    family input into, 73
    flexible seating in, 54–55
    ideal elements of, 50
    importance of, 48
    inclusivity in, 49
    layout of, 50–53
    learning and, 48–49
    outdoor areas, 55
    and psychological environment, 55–56
    wall space, 53–54

physical development, 165
Plutchik, Robert, 19
poverty, 6
prekindergarten, 7, 9, 16, 18, 23, 24, 35, 36, 178
pre-/post-assessments, 131, 155, 156
preschoolers, 13, 50–51, 148
preschool-to-prison pipeline
    and ADHD, 150
    and class environment, 48
    and disciplinary policies, 12
    foundations of, 171
    institutionalized racism and, 9–10
    and opportunity gaps, 25–26
    and unequal treatment, 5, 171
primary emotions, 19, 40
privilege, 30, 71
proficiency, cultural. *See* cultural proficiency
proficiency assessments, 4, 6
protection of self, 15, 18
psychological safety, 55–56, 59

Q
quiet spaces, 47, 57

R
racial groups
    academic outcomes within, 33
    ADHD diagnosis for, 148–149
    equity challenges for, 170
    expulsion rates for, 5–6, 12
    and family-school partnerships, 69
    stereotypes about, 10–11
    unequal treatment of, 4–7, 9
racially and ethnically diverse students
    ACE/trauma effects on, 17
    addressing learning gaps for, 26
    ADHD diagnosis in, 148–149
    age perceptions of, 28
    cultural bias vs., 10–11
    effect of unequal treatment on, 6–7
    exclusionary disciplines for, 5–6, 12, 13–15
    learning gaps for, 6
    low expectations for, 15
    pandemic effects on, 6
    reading/math proficiency of, 4
    in special education, 15–16
racism, 9, 10, 29, 30
    See also institutionalized racism
Rasminsky, Judy, 39
reading assessments, 4
reteaching, 118
Rebora, Anthony, 18
recess, 14
reflection, 169–170
relationship-building
    among peers, 60, 84, 85, 87
    and behavioral considerations, 20, 151
    in family-school partnerships, 67
    and scholastic accommodations, 37
    and UDL roll-out, 115–116
representation, multiple means of
    for assessments, 133
    case study of implementing, 36, 95
    in family-school partnerships, 72
    in lesson plans, 104
    6 E's approach to, 100–101
    and technology, 155, 158–161
    UDL principle of, 33, 35
    and use of wall space, 53–54
resource distribution, 5, 9, 10–11
resources for educators, 181–183
respect, mutual, 58–59
restorative practices, 30
risk taking, 56
Rodriguez-Knutsen, Ana, 10
RoomRecess.com, 163
Rose, David, 34
routines, class
    and ADHD, 150
    flexibility about, 110–112
    and technology, 163
    in temporal environment, 87–88, 89–90, 92
    See also temporal environment

S
safe learning spaces
    in early education, 7–8
    and emotional expression, 33
    five criteria for, 58–59

safe learning spaces (*continued*)
    and meeting of basic needs, 40–42, 57
    mutual trust in, 24–25
    physical classroom as, 48, 56
    and predictability, 110–111
    and school culture, 67–69
    technology in, 164
    and temporal environment, 79
    and triggers, 174
    vs. unsafe, 7
    and unwanted behavior, 79
    and warm demanders, 112
safety, 63
SAMR (Substitution, Augmentation, Modification, and Redefinition) model, 123
scaffolding
    developmentally appropriate, 85
    learning and, 57, 115
    and response to misbehavior, 20–21
    UDL principle of, 34
    varied strategies for, 111
schedule, consistent, 82, 87–88, 89, 92, 111
Schlund, Justina, 24
school culture
    alienation within, 6–7
    and climate, 66
    elements in inclusive, 66, 71, 74–75
    family-school partnerships, 67–69, 70, 74–75
    trust and safety in, 7, 67–69
    of welcome, 41–42, 173
school policy/practices
    antiracist, 172
    developmentally appropriate, 8
    exclusionary discipline in, 13–15
    family input into, 70
    mismatched expectations in, 15
    one-size-fits-all, 23–24
    reinforcing bias in, 42
    systemic inequality in, 4, 5–6, 9, 12, 30
    systemic racism in, 10
    and unequal academic outcomes, 33
school-to-prison pipeline, 3
screen time, 154, 167
seating, flexible, 54–55, 61
secondary emotions, 19, 40
Section 504 Plans, 143–147
security, 63
self-actualization, 42
self-control, 83
self-esteem, 40, 42
    See also academic self-esteem
self-reflection, 32
self-regulation
    and ADHD, 150
    and class layout, 52
    in emotionally-supportive classes, 59
    and student variability, 23
    teacher modeling of, 60
    and the temporal environment, 83
    and trauma, 20
sequence of instruction. *See* temporal environment
Shannon, David, 54
shutting down, 21
singing, 91
6 E's approach, 98
small-group learning, 51, 52, 55
Smith, Mukkaramah, 71
snacks, 57
social-emotional learning
    and academic success, 14
    and antiracism, 30
    and class environment, 48
    criteria for effective, 58–61
    crucial role of early, 7–9, 56–57
    and flexible seating, 55
    four dimensions of, 84
    prioritizing, 28
    student variability and, 77–78
    technology and, 156, 162, 165
    and temporal environment, 80
    and trauma, 18–19
    in welcoming environments, 38, 57–58
social skills, 8, 10–11
Sock Puppets, 160
special education
    and cultural proficiency, 11
    defined, 140

four characteristics of, 140–141
IEP for children in, 141
overidentification for, 9–10, 15–16
referrals to, 37
teacher input into, 146–147
See also Individualized Education Program (IEP)
State of America's Children report, 5
state standard tests, 127
stereotypes, cultural, 10–11
strengths-based approach
to ADHD, 149
to assessments, 125–126, 128, 130–131
in curriculum/instruction, 78, 96
by educators, 175
and eliminating learning barriers, 31
intentionality in, 63
and student variability, 24
via UDL principles, 43
stress
and behavior, 59
fight, flight, and freeze response, 39
toxic, 17–18, 57
structural racism, 10–11
students
as careful observers, 32
early education effects on, 7–9
effect of prejudice on, 4–7, 9
feedback from, 117–118, 178–179
innate needs of, 177
needs as observed by teachers, 142–143
relationship with teachers, 39–40, 85
schedule buy-in from, 111
systemic racism and, 9–10
trauma in the life of, 17–22
triggers for, 174
uniqueness of, 173
variability of, 23
wisdom of, 179
success, academic
among social groups, 33
and family-school partnerships, 68
laid in early years, 8, 14, 37, 170
means for achieving, 175–179

via strengths-based approach, 24–25
and trauma, 17–18
See also academic performance
summative assessments, 122, 124, 126–127, 155
suspension
as ACE/trauma, 17–18
as barrier to learning, 5
and early-life knowledge, 171
effects on students, 13–15
racial/ethnic statistics on, 5–6, 12

T

tardiness, 67
technology
for action/expression, 36, 115
for active learning, 86, 156–157
for assessments, 127, 155–156
class area for, 109
in class materials, 61, 103, 107
and engagement, 98, 115–116
equitable learning and, 153–154
SAMR model for using, 123, 134
tool choice, 157–159
and UDL, 154–157
in a welcoming environment, 49
for young children, 161–166
temporal environment
active learning in, 85–91
designing the, 79–81
importance of, 78–79
inappropriate practices in, 77
social-emotional development in, 84–85
stability in, 79
technology in, 163
and unwanted behavior, 78–79
timers, visual, 82, 84
timing of instruction, 87
See also temporal environment
toxic stress, 17–18, 57
transitions, 80, 90, 92
trauma
ACE effects, 17
and learning, 177
manifestations of, 57
and misbehavior, 18–21, 39

trauma (continued)
    and safe learning spaces, 24–25
    school-based, 17–18, 177
    slow healing from, 40
    and systemic racism, 9–10
    trust and, 39–40
triggers, learning children's, 174
trust
    and basic needs met, 20
    following trauma, 39–40
    in safe learning spaces, 24–25
    in school, 18, 67–69
    in welcoming environments, 62

U

UDL (Universal Design for Learning)
    assessments in, 112–113, 123, 130, 131
    and the brain, 83–84
    case study implementing, 35–37
    in class layout, 52
    clear goals/objectives in, 104–107
    educator collaboration on, 114
    equitable learning via, 33–34, 96, 173
    in family-school partnerships, 72
    guidelines for, 97–98
    how to apply, 96–104, 113–118
    instructional flexibility and, 109–110, 176
    lesson plans informed by, 103–104
    material/resource flexibility and, 107–109
    online resources on, 120
    as strengths-based approach, 43
    technology and, 154–157, 158–161, 162, 167
    three basic principles of, 34–35
    variability in, 87
U.S. Departments of Health and Human Services and Education, 13

V

valuing of students
    vs. mismatched expectations, 15
    student awareness of unequal, 14
    vs. undervaluing, 6
    in welcoming environments, 58–59
    and well-being, 42
variability of students
    assessments and, 124–125, 131
    and families, 68, 69
    and flexible seating, 55
    and learning variation, 35
    and meeting basic needs, 41
    vs. one-size-fits-all curricula, 22–23
    and physical class environment, 49, 50
    policies that reflect, 42–43
    strengths-based approach and, 24
    and technology, 162
    in temporal environment, 81, 82
    UDL and designing for, 34, 119
violence, trauma of, 17
visual timers, 82, 84

W

wall space, use of, 53–54
warm demanders, 112
welcoming environments
    belonging in, 61–62
    in class layout, 47–48, 52–53
    classrooms as families, 75, 173
    criteria for, 58–63
    emotionally, 56–60
    family input into, 69, 71, 73
    and implicit curriculum, 49
    inclusive materials in, 61
    and psychological safety, 55–56
    and school culture/climate, 66
    and social-emotional learning, 38–40
    teacher modeling of, 58
    trauma and, 38–39
    See also physical classroom environment
whole-group learning, 47, 51, 52, 55
working memory, 83, 111
Wynter-Hoyte, Kamania, 71

ABOUT THE AUTHOR

BWEIKIA FOSTER STEEN has dedicated over 25 years to the field of early childhood education. She is currently an associate professor of early childhood education at George Mason University in Fairfax, Virginia. Her research focuses on promoting social, emotional, and academic success among children of color and providing early childhood educators with the practices and strategies to enable this success. Dr. Steen earned her doctorate in international and multicultural education from the University of San Francisco.

www.ingramcontent.com/pod-product-compliance
Lightning Source LLC
Chambersburg PA
CBHW070240090526
44586CB00035B/1077